52
GREAT
BACKGAMMON
TIPS

52
GREAT
BACKGAMMON
TIPS

Kit Woolsey and Patti Beadles

BATSFORD

First published in the United Kingdom in 2007 by
Batsford
10 Southcombe Street
London W14 0RA

An imprint of Anova Books Company Ltd

ISBN: 978 0 7134 9064 0

A CIP catalogue record for this book is available from the British Library.

15 14 13 12 10 09 08 07
10 9 8 7 6 5 4 3 2 1

Reproduction by Spectrum Colour Ltd, Ipswich
Printed by MPG Books Ltd, Bodmin, Cornwall

This book can be ordered direct from the publisher at the website:
www.anovabooks.com
Or try your local bookshop

Contents

Introduction

Backgammon is one of the oldest recorded games. Archeological evidence suggests an early backgammon-like game was played in Sumeria around 2500 BC and backgammon-like games were played by the ancient Romans and Greeks. The game took on its existing form in the 17th century, and except for the addition of the doubling cube in the 1920s has remained largely unchanged.

Most of us get our first introduction to backgammon when we turn over the playing board and wonder what all those funny triangles are for. The more ambitious among us might even read the rules, dig out a pair of dice, and try playing a few games before getting bored and wandering off to do something else. The goal of backgammon is indeed quite simple – to get your checkers (counters) home and take them off the board before your opponent does the same. It sounds easy, even tedious, but in fact backgammon can be a dynamic, fast-paced and exciting game. It can be played socially, in a tournament setting, or as a cut-throat gambling game, and has been described by some as the perfect combination of skill and luck.

Unlike a pure skill game such as chess, it is possible for a novice player to beat even a world-class expert in a single game, though over time the expert's skill will prevail. Backgammon is also a great game for the entire family; it is an excellent way to help children to learn skills in counting, maths, logic and probability, not to mention handling both good and bad luck with grace. Finally, it is also a great way to while away a rainy afternoon.

This book contains strategy basics for beginners, as well as tips to help more advanced players improve their game. The authors are both passionate backgammon players, and hope this book will help you to come to love the game as much as they do.

Rules

Backgammon is a two-player board game. The object is to move all of your checkers to your home board and then take them off before your opponent can do the same.

To begin a game of backgammon, the checkers are set up in the following configuration:

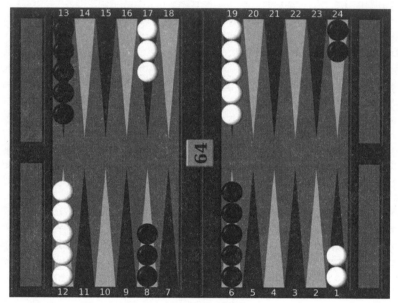

Starting position

The board is divided into four quadrants. In this example, Black's inner or home board is in the bottom right. Black's outer board is in the bottom left. White's outer board is in the top left, and White's home board is in the top right. Black moves his checkers counterclockwise from White's home board to White's outer board, then to Black's outer board and then to Black's home board. White does exactly the opposite, moving from Black's home board to Black's outer board, then to White's outer board and finally to White's home board.

Playing the Game

At the beginning of the game, each player rolls one die. The player who rolled the higher number then moves first, using both the numbers thrown. His opponent then rolls two dice and plays the numbers shown. From then on play alternates until one player has won the game.

On each turn, the player must move checkers according to the number of pips shown on each die. If the player rolls a 5 and a 4, he must move one checker forward five spaces and move one checker four spaces. The same checker can be moved for both parts of the roll, but each number must be moved separately: if it is not possible to play the checker first over either four or five spaces, then the roll cannot be played as a single move of nine spaces. If the roll is doubles, then the player plays the number indicated four times. For example, if the roll is 3-3, then the player plays four moves of three spaces each.

The player must use both (or all four, in the case of doubles) numbers if possible. If not, he must use as many as he can. If the player can play either of the numbers separately but cannot play both, he must play the higher of the two numbers.

A checker can land on any point (triangle marking) that is open, or one that is already occupied by one or more of that player's checkers. If a point is occupied by two or more of the opponent's checkers then a checker may not land in it. If a point is occupied by only one of an opponent's checkers, in this situation called a blot, then the point can be occupied and the opponent's checker removed and placed on the bar (the central partition).

When one or more of his checkers is on the bar, the player must re-enter them on the opponent's home board before he can make any other play. A roll of 1 lets him move onto his opponent's 1-point, a roll of 2 lets him enter on the opponent's 2-point, etc. If the point is blocked, then the player may not enter on that point. If it is occupied by an opponent's blot, then he may enter on that point and the opponent's blot is placed on the bar.

When a player has moved all his checkers to his home board, he begins the process of bearing them off. Rolling a 6 allows him to move one checker from his 6-point, a 5 allows him to remove one from his 5-point, etc. But it is also legal to move a checker the indicated number of spaces rather than bearing one off: if the player rolls a 1, he can either bear a checker off from his 1-point or move a checker one space. If he rolls a large number and there are no checkers on that point or on higher numbered points, he can use that number to remove a checker from the next lowest point available. For example, if he rolls a 6 and there are no checkers on either his 6-point or 5-point, then he can use the 6 to remove a checker from his 4-point.

Doubling Cube

The doubling cube is a relatively recent addition to the game, and allows for the possibility of doubling the score. At the beginning of the game, the doubling cube starts in the centre of the board and each game is worth one point. At the beginning of a player's roll, before the dice are rolled, the player has the option of offering his opponent a double. His opponent then can either decline or accept the double. If the opponent declines the double the game is over, and the player who doubled (offered the double) wins one point. If the opponent accepts, then the cube is placed on his side of the board and the game is now being played for two points instead of one.

Once a player has accepted the cube, he is the only one who can offer a double. Whenever it is his turn, and before the dice are rolled, he may double his opponent. The opponent then has the option of accepting the double and playing for four points, or rejecting the double and losing two points. Once the cube has been turned, only the player who last accepted a double has the right to redouble, and only before he has thrown the dice.

Scoring

The first player to remove all of his checkers scores one point. If his opponent has not yet removed any checkers, then he wins a gammon. If the opponent has not borne any checkers off and still has one or more checkers in the winner's home board, then the winner wins a backgammon. A gammon is worth double points, and a backgammon scores triple points.

If the doubling cube has been turned, then the game value is multiplied by the cube value. For example, if the doubling cube is at 4 and a player wins a gammon, then he scores 4 x 2, or 8 points.

Backgammon Notation

Backgammon notation is a way of describing and recording plays in backgammon. We will use it throughout this book because it provides a simple and precise way of describing a play. While the notation can appear a bit intimidating and technical at first, it is actually very simple and straightforward.

The backgammon board has 24 points (the triangles), 12 on each side of the board. By convention, the farthest point away from you, proceeding anti-clockwise around the board from the bottom left, is called your 24-point (by the same token, it is your opponent's 1-point) and is numbered 24. The numbers then decrease as they go around the board clockwise towards you, until you get to your 1-point, which is numbered 1.

Moves are recorded by listing the roll (the numbers obtained from throwing a pair of dice), followed by the play that was made. For example:

3-1: 8/5 6/5

This says the player rolled a 3 and a 1, and played it by moving one checker from his 8-point to his 5-point, and one checker from his 6-point to his 5-point. In fact, this would be a great play for an opening 3-1 roll.

If the move hits an opponent's blot (exposed checker), then an asterisk is added to the point where the checker was hit:

3-1: 8/5* 6/5

The above move is actually the same as in the previous example, but says that a checker was hit on the 5-point when the play was made.

If the same checker is moved more than once, and no checkers were hit when the play was made, then the interim step is sometimes left out:

6-5: 24/13

The above play says that a checker was moved from the opponent's 1-point out to the midpoint. This move could also be notated as either of the following:

6-5: 24/18 18/13
6-5: 24/18/13

However, if the opponent had a blot on his 7-point (the other player's 18-point), then this play would be written as:

6-5: 24/18*/13
6-5: 24/18* 18/13

When doubles are rolled, multiple checkers are often played to the same location. When this happens, the number of checkers moved to a particular point is written in parentheses:

6-6: 24/18(2) 13/7(2)

This says that two checkers were moved from the 24-point to the 18-point, and two were moved from the 13-point to the 7-point.

Checkers that are played from the bar are either indicated by writing bar or b for the starting point. Checkers that are borne off are either written as off or o:

5-4: bar/20 13/9
5-4: b/20 13/9

6-5: 6/off 5/off
6-5: 6/o 5/o

To practice backgammon notation, set up a board and play a few moves, then after each move write down the play. You will find that the notation very quickly becomes second nature.

Tip 1

Run!

Backgammon is a race. Both players start with their checkers arranged evenly around the board, and then they take turns rolling and moving until somebody gets all their checkers home and takes them all off. The first person to do this wins the game.

The three basic strategy building blocks of backgammon are running, blocking, and hitting. Of these, running is clearly the most important. It is possible to win a game of backgammon without ever hitting one of your opponent's checkers, and also without blocking, although most games feature both hitting and blocking at some point. But you cannot win without taking your checkers off, and you cannot take your checkers off until you run them all home.

When you are ahead in the race, it is often a good idea to adopt a simple strategy of running – you are already winning, and if you just keep running you can often cruise on to victory. Because running games are generally simpler than other types of games, it is harder to make serious mistakes when you are running; there are

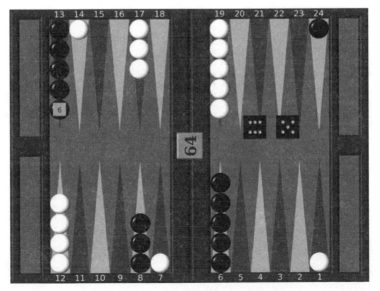

Running game. Black to play 6-5

fewer choices, and the differences between them are smaller. Thus, if you are playing an opponent who is much more skilled than you, it is best to try to play a simple running game and hope you can out-roll him.

The example shown on page 15 is a fairly common early game position. Black opened by rolling 6-5, then White rolled 6-2. Black now rolled 6-5 again, and has a choice to make. There are two plausible plays: 13/7* 6/1* and hit twice, or 24/13. In this case, Black is ahead in the race (he rolled 11 pips on first roll to White's 8, and has now rolled another 11) so there's no reason to complicate the position. Black should just keep running and play 24/13.

Tip 2   Block Your Opponent

Backgammon is inherently a race in which your goal is to run home and then take all of your checkers off the board before your opponent does the same thing. But if that was all there was to it, the game would quickly become a contest to see who could roll better numbers. This would get boring rather quickly, and this book would be very short.

Luckily, however, there is more to backgammon than that. In addition to running, you can also hit your opponent's checkers to send them to the bar, and you can block your opponent's checkers to keep him from running home. Blocking is a very powerful strategy, because it limits your opponent's options and makes it harder for him to get his checkers home.

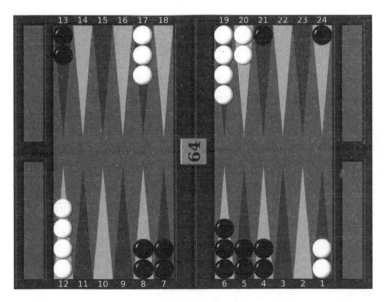

Blocking

In this example, White is in a great deal of trouble. He needs to roll exactly a 6-2 in order to escape one of his back checkers. If he splits his back two checkers to make it easier to escape, then Black will probably hit him and try to close him out, which would be very bad news indeed.

Black, on the other hand, is fairly happy with his position. He has White stuck behind a five-point prime or blockade, whereas Black is free to run home largely unimpeded. If White hits him, then Black should have an easy time getting back on the board and trying to run again.

Tip 3   Hit Your Opponent

The third basic building block of backgammon strategy is hitting. Any time your opponent has a blot (a single checker) on a point, you have the opportunity to hit the blot and send it back to the bar.

When you hit your opponent, several good things happen. The first is that he loses ground in the race, since that checker has to start back at the beginning. Since backgammon is at its essence a race, causing your opponent to lose ground is almost always to your benefit.

Once your opponent is on the bar, on his next roll he must use one of his numbers to come in. That takes away half (or a quarter, if he rolls doubles) of his opportunity to make strategic progress against you. This is called losing a tempo, and is one of the very powerful side effects of hitting.

But wait – things get better! If your opponent is on the bar, there is always a chance that he will completely fail to enter, since he cannot come in on a point that you already occupy with two or more checkers. Backgammon players have a lot of different terms for this – fan, dance, miss, stay on the bar – and it can be incredibly frustrating when it happens to you. But when you hit your opponent and he fails to enter on the next roll, then it is essentially as if you get a free turn.

It is better to hit aggressively than to play too timidly and give your opponent an easy time of it. If you're unsure about whether to hit in a particular situation, do it. When in doubt, hit.

Tip 4

Learn to Build a Prime

If you get one of the powerful opening rolls such as 3-1, 6-1 or 4-2, then you should use them to build points, and you will be well on your way to building a prime.

In the early stages of the game, it is generally correct to make your 5-point, 4-point, 3-point or 7-point if you can do so. If you are not lucky enough to roll so well, then you can at least start the process by bringing one or two checkers down to your 8, 9, 10 or 11-points. These loose checkers are called builders, and you hope to use them very quickly to make points in your prime. It may seem worrying to leave a blot for your opponent to hit, but if your opponent has not moved his back checkers at all, then it will be harder for him to hit a blot in your outer board.

Once you have started to create a prime, you can extend it by building additional points either in front of it or behind it. If you have a choice, it is preferable to build points on the front since points in your home board will also help keep your opponent from

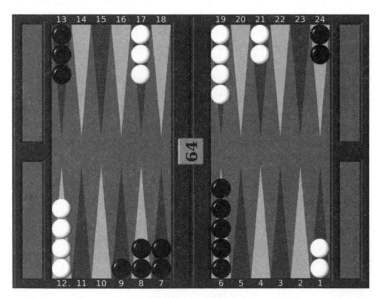

Building primes

getting back on the board if you hit him. Besides, you have to get your checkers home eventually, and doing it early saves you the trouble of doing it later.

If the dice refuse to agree with this strategy, then extending the prime from the back will still keep your opponent locked up in your home board. This strategy is also easier to undertake since you can sometimes add a builder to the back side of your prime, hoping to cover it by adding another checker to the point in a subsequent roll.

In the position shown on the opposite page, both Black and White have started the process of building primes. By leaving a checker at the back edge of his prime, Black is in excellent position to extend his prime on the next roll.

Tip 5   Consider All the Possible Plays

The most common mistake that players make in backgammon, both beginners and more expert players, is overlooking the best play. Once you gain some experience you will often find that when there are multiple good plays, one will just feel 'right' to you, and more often than not that will be the best play.

It is vital to consider all reasonable possibilities before making your play. This is not an easy task, because for any given position and roll there might be over 50 legal plays. While most of these plays will obviously be absurd, it can still take time to weed through the options. But backgammon is a fast-paced game, and if you spend five minutes deliberating over each play you will not be a popular opponent.

Examining your position before you roll will help to narrow down the reasonable moves. You might see that a 2 covers an important blot, while a 3 hits an enemy checker and a 6 jumps over an enemy blockade. Thus, if you roll 3-2, 6-2 or 6-3, it is likely that your play will be the move which achieves two of these good things. If you only roll one of these numbers you are still likely to achieve one good move with that die and make the best possible use of the other die.

However, as in the example on the opposite page, it is important to think of the dice roll as an entire entity, not as two separate pieces. For example, suppose your opponent wins the opening roll with a 6-3 and plays 24/18, 13/10. You then roll a 6-3 back. If you think of the dice roll as two separate pieces you will play 13/7* with the 6 and look around for the best 3 available. But if you look at the entire dice roll you will see that you can play the superior 24/15*, which rips away his builder, sends a third checker back, leaves fewer return shots, gains more in the race and starts to escape a back checker.

In chess, there is a rule that says if you touch a piece you must move it. The same is not generally true in backgammon. In fact, in most games, it is perfectly acceptable for you to make a play, look at it, then put the checkers back in their original positions before trying out one or more additional plays, just to see how they look. You do not commit to a particular play until you pick up your dice.

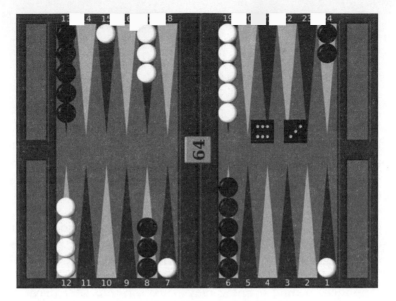

Consider all the possible plays

If there is any doubt in your mind about what the right play is, try out all of the candidate plays first and see how they look. Sometimes you will be surprised that something that looked mediocre in your head turned out to be very good when you saw it on the board – or vice versa.

Tip 6

Learn the Opening Rolls

Every game has an opening roll, and some rolls are much better than others. Good or bad, each roll generally has a best play, or a couple of good ones to choose from. Since doubles are re-rolled for the opening roll, there are only 15 possible opening rolls to consider. It is well worth learning them all, knowing the best plays and whether there is a clearly best play, or the options if plays are close. The starting position is the most common position by far in backgammon, so if you know what to do you are well ahead of the game.

The ideas behind opening plays carry on into later plays. You want to make points, escape the back men, unstack heavy points, diversify your builders and make it difficult for your opponent to play comfortably.

The opening rolls can be grouped as follows:

1) The point-making rolls

> 3-1: Make the 5-point
> 4-2: Make the 4-point
> 6-1: Make the 7 (bar) point
> 5-3: Make the 3-point

These are definitely the best plays. There used to be some question about 5-3 since the 3-point is fairly deep, but it is still a fine asset to have.

2) The sixes

> 6-2: 24/18, 13/11
> 6-3: 24/18, 13/10
> 6-4: 24/18, 13/9 or 24/14 or 8/2, 6/2
> 6-5: 24/13

With the 6, it is definitely better to come out to the enemy bar point rather than slot your own bar point (see Glossary). Even though there are more ways to be hit, getting hit is less costly from this position. In addition, being on the enemy bar point makes your opponent's plays more difficult. With 6-5, of course run to safety; 6-2 and 6-3 are used to bring a builder down from the midpoint to help make an inner board point in the future. This is a good example of working on both sides of the board. 6-4 is also played that way. However, running all the way with 6-4 is fine, since the checker is difficult to hit and is well-placed to work on the offence if missed. Also, making the 2-point, a play that used to be laughed at as a beginner's play, is just about as good. It leads to different types of positions that can be difficult for both sides to play.

3) The aces

   5-1: 24/23, 13/8 or 13/8, 6/5
   4-1: 24/23, 13/9 or 13/9, 6/5
   2-1: 13/11, 6/5 or 24/23, 13/11

With the aces, it is clear to use the non-ace to bring a builder down from the midpoint in order to increase the chances of making an inner board point. The ace can be used either to split the back checkers or to slot the 5-point. Both plays are good. Slotting the 5-point risks getting hit, but it unstacks the heavy 6-point and the 5-point will probably be made next roll if the shot is missed. Splitting the back men increases the chances of making an advanced anchor, as well as making it more dangerous for the opponent to leave a blot in his outer board. With the 4-1, it is generally considered better to split the back men. The reason for this is that the builder on the 9-point gives you so many ways to make a new point next turn that it is probably unnecessary to slot. The 5-1 is a close decision. With the 2-1, it is a little better to slot the 5-point since the checker on the 11-point is 6 away, which is a powerful place to be when fighting for a key point.

4) The rest

   5-4: 24/20, 13/8 or 13/9, 13/8
   5-2: 24/22, 13/8 or 13/11, 13/8
   4-3: 24/20, 13/10 or 24/21, 13/9 or 13/10, 13/9
   3-2: 24/21, 13/11 or 13/10, 13/11

Those rolls that do not make a point and do not contain an ace or a 6 can be played in a variety of ways. For the 5-4, splitting is better than bringing two checkers down. The reason is that after 13/9,

13/8 the position is somewhat cramped, and starting the enemy 5-point before your opponent has had a chance to develop is quite valuable. The various options for the other rolls are all about equal, either bringing two builders down to emphasize the offence or bringing one builder down and splitting the back checkers to work on both sides of the board.

Try all of the various plays so that you become familiar with the types of positions that result from each play. This will give you a better knowledge of how to cope with each of the plays should your opponent win the opening roll. Ultimately, go with the plays that best suit your personal style and taste.

Tip 7   Do Not Play Too Safe

Like many beginners, you may make the mistake of looking for safe plays that do not leave shots (see Glossary for more on shots). This is actually a very short-sighted approach to the game. Although this leaves you safe on the next roll, it is more likely that you will have to leave a shot later in the game. You are also left with less flexibility for building your board and blocking your opponent in.

Novice players often have an irrational fear of getting hit. While getting hit can be bad, it is usually not as horrible as you might think. This is especially true on the first few rolls of the game, when your opponent has not yet built much of a board or a prime and you can just come in again and get back to business.

A perfect example of this is a 5-2 opening roll. The beginner's inclination is to play one checker from the midpoint all the way down to the 6-point. This might seem safe, but it leaves you with six checkers stacked on your 6-point and does nothing at all to improve your strategic position. It is actually much better to either split your back men with the 2, or play a checker from your midpoint to your 11-point. Getting hit this early is no big deal, and if you do not get hit you will have gained a lot more options for your best roll.

Whenever you find yourself building tall towers of checkers, stop and look for a better play. You will almost always find one.

Tip 8   Avoid Getting Trapped

In order to win the game, it is necessary to bring all 15 checkers home. If a back checker or two gets trapped behind the enemy lines, you are not going to win. One of the greatest dangers is having a checker trapped behind a blockade. The checker cannot move, so you are forced to make other, probably undesirable, moves while your opponent calmly brings his men around to bear on the trapped checker. If your opponent is threatening to make a blockade, it is vital to get your back men moving before they get stuck behind the prime.

Proper handling of back checkers can be very difficult. It is very tempting to leave them alone and just work on the offence. Most players have had the experience of splitting their back checkers and then being blown off the board in one roll by a lucky doubles from their opponent. If there is significant danger of a blitz (see Glossary), it is often correct to sit tight. However, getting primed can be just as bad as getting blitzed. You may survive longer, but the result will be the same – a lost game. You need to have a way to escape your back checkers in order to win.

Advancing a back checker is relatively safe when your opponent has little ammunition up front with which to attack. This is why many of the standard opening rolls and responses involve splitting the back checkers. If your opponent is on the bar it is even safer, since he is required to use part of his roll to enter. If you advance a back checker, not only do you have better coverage of his outer board and a good path from which to escape that checker, but you threaten to make an advanced anchor (see entry in Glossary at the back of the book). Once you have an advanced anchor, you are in little danger of being blockaded.

The key factor to consider, when deciding whether or not to advance a back checker, is the structure of your opponent's board. If he has made his bar point, your back checkers are blocked on sixes. Every new point he makes increases the length of his blockade, making it more difficult for you to escape. It is important to get one or both of your back checkers into a position where they can escape with a single roll of the dice. On the other hand, if your opponent has made several inner board points and has builders in place, getting blitzed is a bigger danger than getting trapped. In this situation it is correct to sit tight on his ace point and work on your own offence rather than attempting to leave. Bide your time until your opponent is on the bar, behind a prime of your own or has been forced to break his board.

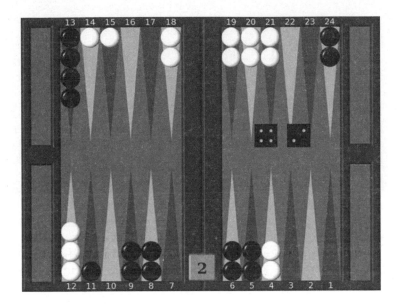

Avoid getting trapped (1). Black to play 4-2

In this position Black is in danger of being trapped. White has a solid four-point prime, and good diversification to extend this prime. In addition White has an advanced anchor, meaning that Black has little chance of trapping White's back checkers, forcing White to break his board. It is vital for Black to prepare to either escape a back checker or make an advanced anchor. Black must play 24/22, 13/9. If Black instead plays 13/11, 13/9, White will probably be able to slot his 8-point, and Black will need to roll very well to escape.

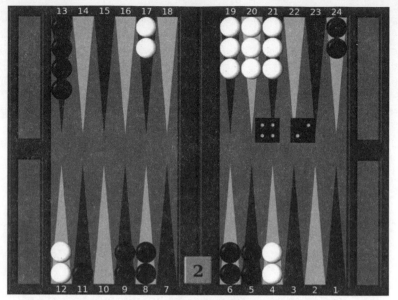

Avoid getting trapped (2). Black to play 4-2

The above is an entirely different situation from the first example. In the first place White does not have his bar point and is unlikely to get it, so Black's back checkers are in no danger of being trapped. They will always be able to escape later with a six. White has four builders trained on his 3-point. If Black plays 24/22, 13/9, he will be asking to be attacked. Instead Black must sit tight with 13/11, 13/9. White may improve his inner board by making his 3- or 2-point, but that will not prevent Black from escaping later if he is able to keep one or both of White's back checkers contained. This time, a blitz from White is the greater danger.

Tip 9   Anchors are Valuable

A defensive anchor, particularly an advanced anchor in your opponent's inner board, is very valuable, and serves the following six purposes:

1) A guaranteed entry place
Regardless of how strong an attack your opponent makes, your anchor guarantees that he cannot close you out completely. You will always have at least one place to enter. Thus the anchor permits you to play more aggressively on other parts of the board, since getting hit is less costly than if you had no anchor.

2) Prime protection
If you are back on the opponent's ace point, it is quite possible for him to construct a full prime to hem these checkers in. However, if you have an advanced anchor on his 4- or 5-point, it is extremely difficult for your opponent to prime these checkers. He simply does not have the ammunition and manoeuvring room, particularly since he starts the game with five checkers on the 6-point.

3) Launching pad
In a priming battle, it is vital to be able to play any roll without breaking your blockade. An advanced anchor provides a launching pad for hit checkers to enter and then jump out into the outfield. If such a checker is hit, it simply enters and escapes again.

4) Outfield coverage
It is advantageous to your opponent to bring builders down from his midpoint into his outer board, in order to make more points. When you are back on his ace point he can do this with relative safety, since at worst he will only be giving you an indirect shot. But if you have an advanced anchor he will be giving you a direct shot if he puts a blot in his outer board. This cramps his play.

5) Shot potential
If you are behind in the race, you need to hit a shot in order to win. When holding an advanced anchor, there is plenty of potential to hit

a shot. You may get an indirect shot when your opponent clears his midpoint. Or you may get a direct shot when he is forced to clear his 8-point or any other outer board point he may have made.

6) Racing potential
If you have an advanced anchor, these checkers are poised to run home if you roll large doubles. A common winning strategy is to grab an advanced anchor, take the lead in the race, and sit and wait for those large doubles. Your opponent cannot do much to prevent this once you have secured that advanced anchor.

However, you cannot hold an anchor forever. In order to win the game, all 15 checkers must be borne off, which means that at some point it will be necessary to abandon the anchor. But since an anchor has so many good things going for it, you should not give up an anchor unless it is advantageous or necessary to do so. A good time to make a run for it with the anchor checkers is when your opponent is on the bar, since he will be unable to attack the remaining checker. If you are way ahead in the race it may be necessary to run off the anchor, since often the only alternative will be to wreck your offensive structure. If you roll big doubles, this is often the opportune time to move both checkers from the anchor in one move. But in general you do not want to give up an advanced anchor lightly.

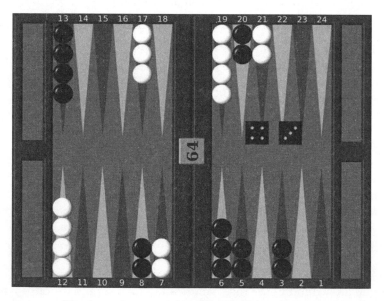

Black anchor position (1). Black to play 4-3

Black could seize this opportunity to run one back checker to safety with 20/13, but he should hold the anchor and play the comfortable 13/6. Black is not in too much danger of being attacked if he runs, since he has the stronger inner board and White is short on attacking ammunition. But Black is only just ahead in the race, so even if he succeeds in escaping the other back checker he will still have a long way to go to win the game.

But Black has time to wait and see what happens. By playing 13/6 he gives himself the option of either running later if he rolls big doubles or, if White rolls the big doubles first, sitting on the anchor and getting a shot.

Now, look at the same position, but put two of the checkers on Black's midpoint onto his 6-point:

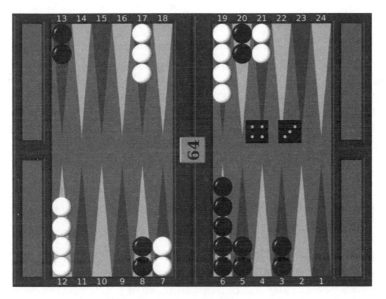

Black Anchor Position (2). Black to play 4-3

This time Black should make a run for it with 20/13. Now he is well ahead in the race, so if he escapes his other back checker he will be in a good position. In addition, Black is running out of decent moves. If he does not run he will have either to give up his 8-point or play deep in his board with 6/3, 6/2; both options are unattractive. For Black, this is an opportune time to give up the anchor and get a badly needed spare checker onto the midpoint so that he can handle his future rolls. If however Black stubbornly holds onto the anchor, his position will probably just continue to deteriorate.

Tip 10   Every Point Helps

Every point you make has the potential to be a valuable asset, regardless of where the point is or whether it is doing any immediate good. Once the point is made, it stays made; your opponent cannot take it away from you until either you voluntarily release it or the dice force you to release it.

A made point has several potential uses:

1) A blocking point
If you own the point, your opponent cannot move onto it. This may restrict him in his choice of moves. Even a sole outfield point may prove to be a critical stumbling block for your opponent if he rolls a number that would otherwise play comfortably if the point were not there. An inner board point is potentially even more valuable, since it helps prevent a hit checker from entering.

2) A landing place
Your checkers need safe places to go to, in particular after your opponent has built up his board. A made point provides such a landing place.

3) Communication
If you do not have points, there is a danger that your opponent can form a 6-point prime and trap one or more of your checkers. A point high in his inner board, such as his 4- or 5-point, or a point in his outer board prevents this, and also keeps your checkers in communication with one another. For example, suppose you own his bar point. If one of your checkers gets hit, once it enters anywhere it is threatening to hop out to his bar point. From there it can continue on its way around the board when the right number appears.

4) For covering territory
Every point you have made covers the area in front of it. An enemy checker that lands six or fewer pips in front of the point is exposed to a direct shot. And if you have a third checker on the point, you can hit without releasing the point.

Since points are so valuable, you should not pass up chances to make new points unless there is something more valuable to do with those checkers. Likewise, once a point is made you should not release it lightly. Even if the point does not appear to be valuable at present, it may become very important in the future. As long as there is significant contact, with both players having men back, "any point in the storm" is valuable.

In fact, the more points the merrier, because two points next or close to each other form part of what may become a prime. Also, they provide multiple landing places for your checkers. And if the points are on the enemy side of the board, they present difficulties for your opponent as he tries to come home safely.

Consider the following scenario: At the start of the game, you own your 6, 8, 13 and 24-points. You want to get off the 24-point when convenient, since those two checkers may become trapped otherwise. The other points are valuable, so you do not want to give them up without good reason. Your goal is to build more points as the dice permit, and to place your checkers so as to maximize your chances of building more points. The points that you build will eventually come into play, and you will be glad that you have them.

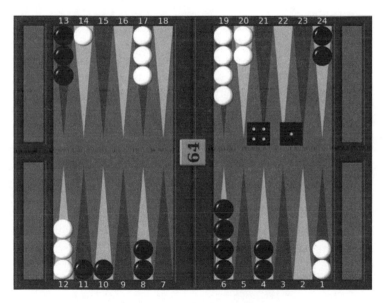

Make points. Black to play 4-1

The bar point is a valuable point, particularly when your opponent has two checkers on your ace point. The bar point blocks these checkers from moving with a 6, which is very important. In the above situation, many players would make the bar point with this 4-1 roll. The problem with that play is that it releases the 8-point. The 8-point is not currently blocking White's back checkers, but once they start moving the 8-point will become quite valuable. In addition, making the bar point leaves two outfield blots. Black is better off playing 13/9, 10/9. This gives him four points on his side of the board instead of just three. If Black can then make either his 5-point or his bar point, he will have a formidable blockade. It is true that neither the 9-point nor the 8-point by itself is as valuable as the bar point in this position, but holding both of them is stronger than just having the bar point.

Tip 11   Have a Game Plan

There is so much more to backgammon than just racing checkers around the board. Think instead of the checkers as two conflicting armies that can be played strategically to block, or hit, opposing checkers. Moves must be made with a purpose, and you should always have a game plan in mind.

There are several possible plans – some are short range, others are long range. These plans are not mutually exclusive, but should work together, and a skilled player may have several different plans in action. In addition, it is a good idea to keep various options open, so that you can opt for the plan indicated by the dice. Short-range plans might include hitting an enemy blot, making a new point, playing safe or escaping a back checker. Long-range plans might entail bringing all 15 men home, building a prime to block enemy checkers, running a blitz, or adjusting timing for a priming battle or a back game.

Unlike a game such as chess, you are at the mercy of the dice; you may not be able to carry out your intended game plan if the dice refuse to cooperate. You must be prepared to switch plans at a moment's notice if that is what the dice imply. Sticking stubbornly with the same plan can lead to ruin. To be successful in backgammon you must choose your plan to be consistent with both the actual state of play, and with what the dice have given you to work with.

A particular example of this is the race. The player who is ahead in the race is a favourite to win the game provided no checkers are hit. Therefore, if you are ahead in the race your plan should be to disengage your checkers from the enemy and turn the game into a straight race. In contrast, if you are behind in the race you should attempt to keep as much contact as possible in the hope of hitting a shot later. As a rule, race when you are winning, and attack or prepare to attack when you are losing.

The state of the race can change significantly on a single roll of the dice. Many games are close races, where the pip count only differs by a small amount. If either side rolls a large double or hits an advanced checker then the race may shift significantly. You should pay attention to this and be prepared to alter your game plan to match the new circumstances.

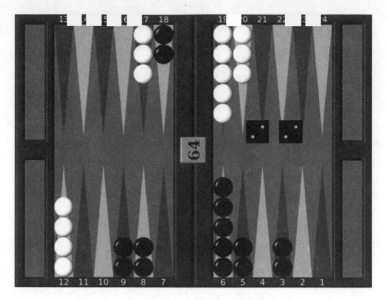

Game planning. Black to play 2-2

Black can make a beautiful prime by playing 9/7(2), 6/4(2). However, his correct play is 18/14(2). Black is already ahead by 5 pips before playing, and after this roll he will be ahead by 13 pips. He is ahead in the race, so he should race. After playing 18/14(2) he will merely need to roll two numbers larger than 2 to move both back checkers and turn the game into a straight race, which is his proper game plan.

Tip 12 When in Doubt, Hit

One of your most powerful weapons is the hit, because hitting an enemy blot achieves many wonderful things:

1) Hitting gains in the race
Whenever you hit an enemy blot, you send that checker back to the bar. Since the bar is in essence the zero point, you have gained whatever number of pips that checker has been sent back. For example, if you hit an enemy checker on your opponent's bar point, you have gained 18 pips in the race. Since backgammon always comes down to a race, thinking of it this way is very important.

2) You put the opponent on the bar
The rules of the game require that a checker on the bar must be entered before any other play can be made. If your opponent is unable to enter, he forfeits his entire roll, which is excellent for you. Even if you own only your 6-point, there is still a 1 in 36 chance that your opponent will roll 6-6 and not be able to enter. Each additional inner board point you make greatly increases the chances that your opponent will be unable to come in, and will stay on the bar if hit, thus making hitting even more powerful.

3) You deprive your opponent of half of his roll
If your opponent has a checker on the bar he must enter, so unless he rolls doubles he can play only one other checker elsewhere. This means that he cannot make a new offensive point. If he is not on the bar a 3-1 roll will make the 5-point for him, but if he is on the bar that possibility will not be available. Restricting his options in this manner is very valuable. You can play much more freely when your opponent is on the bar, since he can do less damage when half of his roll is taken away from him.

4) You rip away a builder
If an opponent has a checker in his outer board, he can use that checker to help make valuable points. By hitting that checker you take away the builder, thus slowing up your opponent's development.

5) You kick him off a key point
Often your opponent has left the checker on a point that he would very much like to make. By hitting, you prevent him from making the point.

6) You start a point of your own
If the hit checker is on an important point, you can use your checker as your own initial effort to make that point. Since your opponent is on the bar he will be limited in his ability to hit back, so you are more likely to be successful.

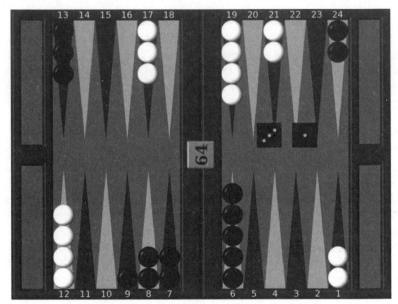

Hitting (1). Black to play 3-1

In the above example Black could make his 5-point, of course. But if he does so, White is likely to make his own 5-point. Then Black will be at a small disadvantage, since White will be better developed. Black should instead play 24/20*. In addition to the big racing gain, this prevents White from making the 5-point without a very lucky roll. Also, Black is starting White's 5-point, a point Black would very much like to make. So now it is Black who has the advantage.

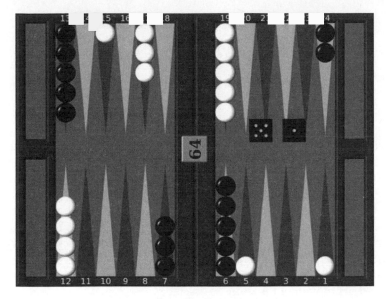

Hitting (2). Black to play 5-1

Here, Black could play quietly with 24/23, 13/8, which is a good way to play an opening 5-1. White's checker on Black's 5-point changes things. Now Black must hit with 13/8, 6/5*. This stops White from making Black's 5-point, and simultaneously Black threatens to make his own 5-point. In addition, by hitting Black takes away half of White's roll. This means that, on his next turn, White will be unable to make use of the builder on his 10-point to make an inner board point. It is true that White will have a lot of rolls that could hit back on Black's 5-point, but as yet he has not rolled one of the hitting numbers. If White fails to hit back, Black will be a favourite to make his 5-point and have a good position.

Naturally, hitting is not always the best option. Sometimes hitting is too dangerous, since it may involve breaking a crucial anchor. Sometimes it is more important to make an offensive point. But, generally, when in doubt, hit.

Tip 13   Keep Your Checkers in Play

You resources in backgammon are limited: you have only 15 checkers with which to manoeuvre and, in addition, the rolls of the dice will restrict the plays that you can make. With such limited resources, it is important to hoard your checkers and keep every one in play.

Checkers cannot move backward unless they are hit and sent to the bar. Once a checker is moved to a point, it can only move forward from that point – never backwards. For checkers in the outfield this is not a problem, since these checkers have plenty of room to go forward. But once a checker is placed in your inner board, its movement is quite restricted:

> A checker on the 6-point can no longer be moved with a 6.
> A checker on the 5-point can no longer be moved with a 6 or a 5.
> A checker on the 4-point can no longer be moved with a 6, 5 or 4.
> A checker on the 3-point can no longer be moved with a 6, 5, 4 or 3.
> A checker on the 2-point can no longer be moved with a 6, 5, 4, 3 or 2.
> A checker on the 1-point cannot move at all.

The deeper a checker goes into the inner board, the fewer options this particular checker has. So, ideally, you want to keep your spare checkers as far back in your inner board as possible to provide more flexibility. In particular, you want to avoid playing behind an enemy anchor, since you want all your checkers aimed at the anchor when your opponent is finally forced to leave it. It is okay to make deep points in your inner board, if you must, but do not leave blots back there unless there are no other palatable options. It is better to make the higher points, of course, since the higher points serve as blocking points, good landing points and good places for spares which you need to swallow bad rolls. And at least the low points help when your opponent is on the bar, but a third checker on a low point cannot be of any use, or even move.

So avoid burying checkers on low points if at all possible; trying to play with buried checkers is like fighting with one hand tied behind your back, whereas you need all your resources to win the game. It is well worth taking some risks in order to keep all checkers in play. Just remember that your checkers cannot move backwards, and that once a checker is buried, it is dead forever.

When you watch a weak player, you will often see his game deteriorate as one checker after another heads for low points and he cannot find any good plays. This seldom happens to the expert, who strives to keep his checkers in play – he somehow seems to have the spare checker he needs in order to move, no matter what he rolls.

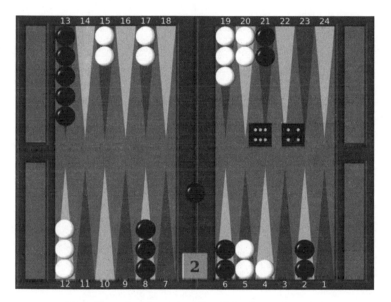

Keeping checkers in play. Black to play 6-4

Here, Black must enter with the 4, and for the 6 he must choose between 13/7 and 8/2. 13/7 leaves a double direct shot, and Black will not be happy if he is hit. But 8/2 is exactly the sort of play that should be avoided if at all possible. Black can live with the two checkers that are already on the 2-point, but putting a third checker would be terrible, since that checker would be virtually out of play for the rest of the game. The only way it could move would be if Black was to roll an ace, and then it could only move to the ace point, which is no bargain. In addition, 8/2 would strip Black's 8-point and leave him with a totally inflexible position. 13/7 is better. If White misses the shot, which he will almost half the time,

Black has a good chance of being able to cover the blot and make his bar point, or to use the checker on the bar point to make a new inner board point. If White does hit, the situation is not so good, but since White only has a 2-point board, Black reckons to enter quickly, and at least the checker will be in play after being hit. Then it can be used to make a new point, to hit one of White's blots, or just as something to move if Black rolls a bad number – and that is a lot better than dumping a third checker onto the 2-point, where it will probably rot for the rest of the game.

Tip 14

Do Not Volunteer Shots Unnecessarily

There is a motto in the army, 'don't volunteer', and this is often true in backgammon as well. While sometimes you are forced to leave direct shots, usually you should avoid leaving shots when there is no need to. It can be quite costly to get hit – not only do you lose ground in the race, but you get stuck on the bar and are forced to take half of your next roll to enter. If you are unable to enter, you lose your full roll. In addition, that returning checker becomes another back checker that needs to be brought around, and is a missing checker from your offence.

In the early stages of the game it is worth taking some risks in order to improve your board. When your opponent has no inner board points other than his 6-point, getting hit is not too serious. You reckon to enter quickly, with time to reorganize. Thus, plays like slotting your 5-point from the heavy 6-point with an ace are often correct, because the gain from making your 5-point is considerable, while being hit is far from fatal. At this point the game is young, so you will have time to recover from the loss in the race.

But as the game develops, volunteering shots in this way becomes more dangerous. Your opponent is building up his board, and there is a greater danger of having a hit checker stuck on the bar or trapped behind a blockade. At this stage, it is important to play carefully and safely, particularly if you have the advantage and are ahead in the race. Getting hit at this stage will turn the game around.

In the example on page 46, there are many players who would put it all on the line with 13/9, 13/8, but this would be misjudged. White's board is perfect, and getting hit means that Black will probably lose the game. Black can afford to wait, and his proper play is 6/2, 6/1. He should leave the spare checker on the 8-point in case he rolls a six. If he moves this checker in he is forced to leave a shot with 6-1, and forced to vacate the 8-point with other 6s, after which a 6 will squeeze him off the midpoint. By waiting, Black gives himself a chance to roll 2-2, 3-3, 4-4 or 5-5, and to clear the midpoint without leaving a shot. He reckons to having a few rolls to wait before getting squeezed off the midpoint. If Black fails to roll those doubles he may roll another 5-4 or 5-3 later, and then bring the checkers down.

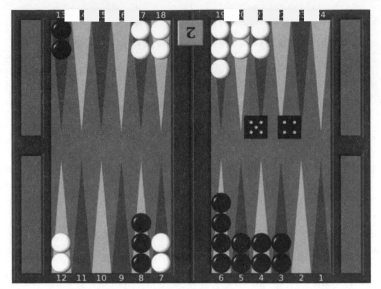

Avoiding unnecessary volunteering (1).
Black to play 5-4

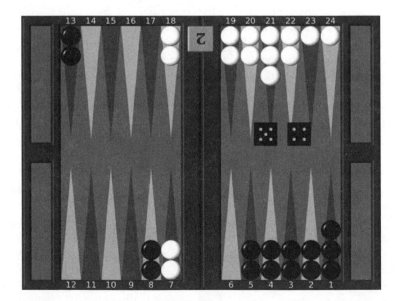

Avoiding unnecessary volunteering (2).
Black to play 5-4

The above is a probable resulting position where Black tried to hold on and then failed to roll the necessary doubles. This time, he should play 13/9, 13/8 with the 5-4. If he instead delays the evil day by playing 8/4, 8/3, things are likely to get worse. 13/8, 13/11 leaves White only 11 shot numbers (all 2s), but if Black waits and then is forced to run one checker from the midpoint, he will leave 17 shot numbers (all 6s, 5-1, 4-2, 3-3 and 2-2). If Black rolls 5-1 next he will be forced to leave a double shot. Also White has two blots in his inner board that he might not manage to cover quickly, so if Black is hit he has one shot to hit back and get back in the game.

Tip 15   Understand the Jacoby Rule and Other Special Rules

It is a good idea to become familiar with the various special rules that are sometimes used in backgammon. That way, if an opponent wants to use them you will be informed, and able to agree or disagree as you wish.

The most important rule is the Jacoby rule. It says that the winner of a game cannot score a gammon or a backgammon unless the doubling cube has been offered and accepted during the game. This rule is used to speed up the game and keep it interesting, and saves time in situations where one player is guaranteed to win, but has only a small chance of winning a gammon. The Jacoby rule forces him to double and go straight on to the next game.

Playing with the Jacoby rule requires only minor strategy adjustments. If you are in a situation where you are winning, and there is a reasonable chance that you could quickly get your opponent into a scenario where he is likely to get gammoned, then you should double before that happens, so that you have the opportunity to win a doubled game.

A less common rule is to allow beavers. A beaver allows a player who is being doubled the opportunity to turn the doubling cube again and still maintain control of the cube. When this happens, the player who initially offered the double can reject the beaver and lose the stakes that he doubled to, or he can accept the beaver and play at four times the stakes from before the initial double. It is relatively uncommon for a beaver to be a correct play, because it means that you believe your opponent has made a serious mistake in offering you the double, and that you are actually favoured to win the game.

Some players like to play with a rule called automatics or automatic doubles. As already explained, at the start of a game each player rolls one die and the player who rolls the higher die plays that roll. However, if both players roll the same number, they pick up the dice and try again. When automatic doubles are in effect, if both players roll the same number then the doubling cube is turned to 2 before re-rolling, and the game starts out at double the usual stakes. This serves no strategic purpose, but simply allows you to 'gamble it up' from time to time.

The Jacoby rule is almost always used when playing for money, while beavers and automatics are less common. None of these rules are ever used in match or tournament play. You should discuss these rules with your opponent before starting to play, in order to avoid confusion.

Sometimes in friendly games your opponent will want to play with nonstandard rules. There are quite a variety of these, and it would be impossible to list them all here. A couple of the more common ones are:

1) On the opening roll, the winning player rerolls the dice before making his move. This allows doubles to be played as an opening roll.

2) No more than five checkers can be stacked on a single point.

You will never encounter such rules in tournament or other serious play. In friendly games, it's best to agree on nonstandard rules before starting to play, but your opponent may not know that his rules are out of the ordinary. If you encounter a nonstandard rule in the middle of a game, the only thing you can do is to reach a gentleman's agreement in the most gracious manner possible.

Tip 16   Play Bots

Have you ever wanted to play backgammon, but found that none of your friends were interested? Do you find yourself craving a quick game of backgammon before bed? Would you like to have an expert tutor available to you any time of the day or night? If so, you might enjoy playing playing against the computer.

Thanks to pioneering research by Gerry Tesauro of IBM, computer programs have learned to play backgammon with the same skill as world-class experts. Playing against a computer program, or 'bot', has a number of advantages: a bot never has other plans, never gets tired and will not complain if you get a lucky roll. Bots that play backgammon are available whenever you want them, for as long as you want, and they do not mind if you get bored and quit in the middle of a game. They can generally be set to play at a variety of skill levels, from beginner to expert, so you are guaranteed to find one that matches your skill. If you want the toughest competition possible, set the bot to expert level. If you would rather have a fighting chance, pick an easier level.

In addition, many backgammon bots have tutoring capability built in. They can tell you what the best move is, what the other reasonable moves are and how much of a difference there is between them. This is a powerful tool for improving your game; it is as if the best player in the world is sitting right next to you, correcting you whenever you make a mistake. One particular bot, Gnu Backgammon, plays at a world-class level, has powerful tutoring and analysis tools, and is completely free. You can download it at http://gnubg.org

Tip 17   Play Online

Another possible solution to having nobody to play backgammon with is to play online. There are numerous internet sites where you can find a game. A few of these can be used from within a web browser, but most require you to install their custom client software. Either way, the site should have good instructions for getting you started. Once you get the client software you can create a new account, choose a username, and then start playing – all this is generally quite a simple procedure. While a few sites charge a membership fee, most are completely free. Many online sites offer the chance to play for money, but do watch out – online backgammon is fast-paced, and can be addictive.

Most sites have a ratings system of some sort that will give you a feel for how good you are and can help you find opponents at a similar skill level. Ratings systems are often based on the FIBS (First Internet Backgammon Server) ratings formula, which in turn is based on the Elo system that is used in chess. In the FIBS system, new players start out at a rating of 1500, and then either gain or lose rating points according to a complex formula that takes into account their skill, their opponent's skill and the length of the match. You win more points for beating a highly rated player than a lower-rated one, and longer matches are worth more points than short ones.

On most servers you can chat with your opponents, chat with other users of the site and also watch other players' matches. Watching highly skilled opponents is an excellent way to improve your game. Some sites also offer special features like tournaments, ladders, leagues and special events.

Tip 18   Learn to Count Shots

If you are considering leaving a shot, or are forced to leave a shot, it is helpful to know that the chances of it being hit by your opponent. Counting shot numbers may seem like a laborious task, but with a few shortcuts it actually becomes very easy.

For a start, there are 36 possible rolls of the dice, each equally likely. Why is this? Picture two dice, one red and one green. The red die can come up as anything from 1 to 6 (that is, six possibilities), and the same is true for the green die. Thus, there are 36 possible combinations in total – each of the six red die possibilities times each of those for the green die. Note that for non-doubles, each possibility comes up twice, since for a 6-4, say, it could be red 6, green 4 or green 6, red 4.

The possible dice rolls can be represented graphically as follows:

```
1-1  1-2  1-3  1-4  1-5  1-6
2-1  2-2  2-3  2-4  2-5  2-6
3-1  3-2  3-3  3-4  3-5  3-6
4-1  4-2  4-3  4-4  4-5  4-6
5-1  5-2  5-3  5-4  5-5  5-6
6-1  6-2  6-3  6-4  6-5  6-6
```

Suppose that you leave a single direct shot – an ace, say. Of the 36 rolls, how many of them contain a one? By looking at the chart above, you can easily see that there are 11 – the 1s on the top and the 1s on the left side. Note that it is 11, not 12, since 1-1 occurs only once. This gives the probability of being hit as 11/36.

You could say that, since each die has a 1 in 6 probability of being a 1, it seems as though the probability of being hit with an ace is 1/6 + 1/6 = 1/3 (or 12/36). But that is incorrect, since it would double count 1-1, which has an ace on both die. To look at it another way, consider the probability of *not* being hit. That needs a non-ace on the red die, and a non-ace on the green die. The probability of a non-ace on the red die is 5/6, as is the probability of a non-ace on the green die. To *not* be hit, the probability is 5/6 x 5/6 = 25/36. This is consistent with the probability of being hit being 11/36.

What about a double shot, for instance two blots 1 and 2 spaces away? Counting the rolls in the upper two rows and the two leftmost columns gives 20 of the 36 rolls. To see if this is correct, work out the probability of being missed. That would mean a non-hitter on the red die, probability 4/6, and a non-hitter on the green die, probability 4/6. 4/6 x 4/6 = 16/36, which is the probability of *not* being hit, so 20/36 is indeed the probability of being hit. Note that if you leave a double shot, you are more likely than not to get hit.

The calculations on the ace would be true for any single direct shot, if it required exactly that roll of the dice to hit with. But there may also be combinations. For example, what is the probability of being hit with a checker that is six away, if there are no points in the middle to block the shot? We start will all 6s, 11 rolls. Also there is 5-1, 4-2, 3-3 and 2-2. Note that 5-1 and 4-2 get counted twice, since they are non-doubles, as it might be 5 red, 1 green or 1 red, 5 green. That comes to a total of 17 shot numbers.

To count any multiple shot scenario, simply count the individual shots from each checker, making sure to avoid double counting. Keep in mind that any direct shot has 11 numbers – this simplifies the counting considerably. For example, suppose there are aces and fives to hit with. How many shot numbers? For a start there are 11 aces. Then there are 11 5s, but 5-1 and 1-5 have already been counted so there are only 9 additional 5s. That brings the total so far to 20 possibilities. In addition there is 3-2 (and also 2-3, of course), for a grand total of 22. It is as simple as that.

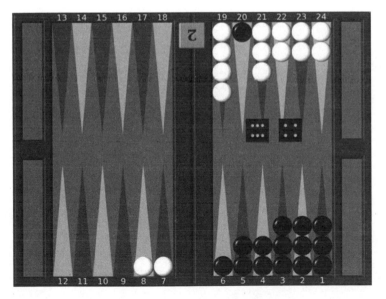

Counting shots. Black to play 6-4

In this scenario Black must play 20/14 with the 6. Should he keep going? Your intuition might say no, since that would be walking into a double shot. But let's count the shot numbers.

If Black plays 20/10, White hits with all 2s and 3s, which as we have seen is 20 shot numbers. There is also the combination of 1-1, getting up to 21 shot numbers out of 36.

If Black plays 20/14, 6/2, White hits with all 6s and 7s. As we have seen, there are 17 shot numbers with a 6, the 11 direct hits and the 6 combinations from 5-1, 4-2, 3-3 and 2-2. For the 7s, there is 6-1, 5-2 and 4-3. 6-1 has already been counted, so we avoid double counting that. That leaves 5-2, 2-5, 4-3 and 3-4 for 4 additional shot numbers, coming to a total of 21 shot numbers. Since this is exactly the same number of shots as 20/10 leaves, it is clearly better to play 20/10, since if Black is missed he is almost certainly home free.

Tip 19 Learn to Count Pips

In backgammon it is often valuable to know who is currently winning, and by how much, because to a large extent your playing strategy will be determined by the status of the race. If you are ahead, you want to do whatever is necessary to stay ahead. While you have no control of where the dice fall, you can choose to play safer and avoid leaving shots, and prioritize escaping any remaining back checkers. Providing you are not hit or hemmed in, your racing lead will often hold up and allow you to coast on to victory. But if you are behind in the race, the opposite is true – you need to do something to equalize the race. This means either hitting an enemy checker or hemming in one of your opponent's checkers so it is unable to move. In this scenario you are less concerned about being hit yourself, or being blocked in, since you are already behind.

The best way to find out who is winning is to count pips. In addition, the pip count can be very important for cube decisions, particularly in a straight race. In backgammon, a pip count is the number of points that you have to roll in order to take all of your checkers off. (A pip is a single spot on the dice.) Counting pips takes some work, but it gets easier with practice.

To count pips, imagine that the board is numbered 1 to 24, with 1 being the 1-point of your home board, and 24 being the 1-point of your opponent's home board. Multiply the number of checkers on each point by the number of that point and then add up the total, and you will have your pip count. Now pretend that you are sitting on your opponent's side of the board and do the same thing for his checkers – by comparing the two counts you will know who is currently winning.

For example, imagine the starting position. There are two checkers on your opponent's 1-point, which works out as 24 x 2, or 48. There are five checkers on the midpoint, which is numbered 13, working out to 65. Adding the two pip counts so far gives 65 + 48 = 113. There are three checkers on the 8-point. 3 x 8 = 24, plus the 113 so far makes 137. And finally, there are five checkers on the 6-point, bringing 5 x 6 = 30, plus the 137 so far makes 167. In fact, the pip count at the start of the game is 167-167 (obviously, the same for both players).

Most backgammon software and online backgammon sites provide the pip count as part of the board display while you are playing. Get into the habit of looking at it on each roll, and think about the pip count as part of your strategy. Ask yourself, are you winning or losing the race? How big is the difference between you and your 'opponent'? Doing this will improve your play, and you will start to get an intuitive feel for the pip count just by looking at the position.

As you become more experienced you will find that you rarely need to take a pip count in practice. Instead you will usually have a good feel for who is ahead or behind, and will choose your plays accordingly. But if you do need to take a pip count, it is helpful to know just how to do so quickly and accurately.

Tip 20   Learn Faster Ways to Count Pips

Counting pips seems hard, and can be slow. There are shortcuts that can help you estimate the race much more quickly than counting every pip for each side.

Counting crossovers is one way to get a good approximation of the race, and is much faster than counting pips. A crossover is the movement of a checker from one quadrant of the board to the next. A checker in your home board takes one crossover to bear off. A checker in your outer board takes two: one to get to your home board and then one to bear off. A checker in your opponent's outer board takes three, while one in your opponent's home board takes four.

In the starting position, you have two checkers in your opponent's home board for a crossover count of 8. There are five checkers in your opponent's outer board, 5 x 3 = 15; adding the previous subtotal, 8, to this gives 23. Continuing in this manner, there are three checkers in your outer board, 3 x 3 = 9; adding 23 to this gives 32. Finally there are five checkers in your home board, 5 x 1 = 5, plus 32 gives a grand total of 37.

Another way to count pips is to count the difference between the two sides of the board. Counting the total number of pips for each side means a lot of addition, and plenty of room for error. Fortunately, you do not need to know the total number of pips for both players in most cases. It is the difference between the pip counts that is important, because this will tell you whether you are ahead or behind in the race, and by how much. Consequently, simply taking the difference between the pip counts of the two players will suffice.

As an example of what this entails, suppose Black has five checkers on his 6-point and White has four checkers on his 6-point. There is no need to count 30 for Black and 24 for White, instead you can simply count 6 for Black, because the remaining checkers cancel each other out. In this way you are generally dealing with smaller numbers. In addition, you do not have to keep track of two separate pip counts – one number is all you need, and you simply add or subtract in relation to that number as you count the difference between the checkers on each side. Consider the following position:

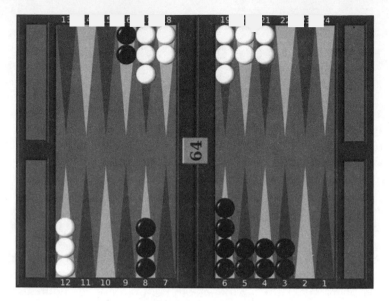

Counting pips

In this example, if you counted directly you would get:

Black has 2 x 3 (6) + 2 x 4 (8) + 2 x 5 (10) + 4 x 6 (24)
+ 3 x 8 (24) + 2 x 16 (32) = 104
White has 2 x 4 (8) + 2 x 5 (10) + 3 x 6 (18) + 2 x 7 (14)
+ 3 x 8 (24) + 3 x 13 (39) = 113

What a lot of work! And plenty of opportunity to make a mistake.

By comparison, here is the simpler way, which only looks at the difference between Black and White. Starting from the lowest points: Black has two extra checkers on the 3-point, so that makes 6. The 4- and 5-points cancel each other out. Black has 1 extra on the 6-point, so that brings the tally up to 12 (by adding 1 x 6). But White has two extra checkers on the bar point for 14, so that comes to -2 (from 12 - 14). The checkers on the 8-points cancel. Black has two checkers 3 farther away than White's outfield checkers, so that is 6 for Black, bringing the subtotal to 4 (from -2 + 6). And White has one checker, as yet unaccounted for, on the midpoint for 13, for a final total of -9 (from 4 – 13). The result is the same as the first method, where the difference would be obtained by comparing totals (in this case 104 – 113 = -9) but there was only one number to remember during the addition, and no large numbers or groups of numbers to deal with. So if Black now rolls, say, 6-5 he knows it is right to run the back checkers and turn the game into a straight race.

Tip 21　Fill in Gaps When Bearing In

There is an old backgammon saying, 'You can't take them off until you bring them home'. This certainly applies when scrambling to get off a gammon, but when trying to win a straight race for the game, it can be another story. Remember, it is not the player who takes the first checker off who wins; it is the player who takes his last checker off first. Consequently, when bringing your men home in a straight race it is important to place these checkers so as to maximize your chances of getting off as quickly as possible.

You cannot play more pips than the dice let you play. If your remaining checkers total 63 pips, you cannot take them all off until you have rolled a total of 63 pips or more on the dice, no matter how you play your moves. If you are able to always move all of your pips, you will have done the best you can.

You should try to avoid a situation where you are unable to play the full pips on the dice. You can lose pips when you roll a number larger than any inner board point that you have checkers on. For example, suppose one of your dice is a 6, but you do not have any checkers on your 6-point. The best you can do is bear a checker off from the 5-point using the 6, but you will have wasted a pip. Of course you are hardly complaining about having rolled the 6, but if you had got a checker on the 6-point you would not have wasted that pip. This indicates that when you bear in you should try to put several checkers onto your 6-point in order to avoid wasting with a 6.

In the previous example you wasted one pip from having to play a 6 from the 5-point. It can get a lot worse than this when you have a group of checkers on a low point. As an extreme example, suppose you have left just three checkers on the ace point. That is only 3 pips in total, but you need doubles (giving you four separate numbers to move) to take them off all at once. If you do not roll doubles, you can only move 2 pips in total (1+1) regardless of what numbers you roll. A roll of 6-5 will therefore waste 9 pips. Consequently, it is very bad to have a group of checkers on the low points in a race. You should bear in on the high points.

There is yet another problem. Suppose you have several checkers on the 6-point, but no checkers on the 5-point. If you roll a 5, you will have no choice but to play 6/1 with the 5, putting a checker onto the ace point – exactly where you do not want it. If you roll several 5s before clearing the 6-point, you will be forced to put a lot of checkers onto the ace point. As shown in the previous scenario, these checkers will later lead to wastage. Similarly, if your 4-point is empty and you have men on the 5- and 6-point, a roll of a 4 forces you to put a checker deep onto the ace or 2-point. Consequently, it is important to put a few checkers on each of the 6- and 5-points if you can, in order to avoid this possible wastage. Having a smooth position is more important than bringing men home.

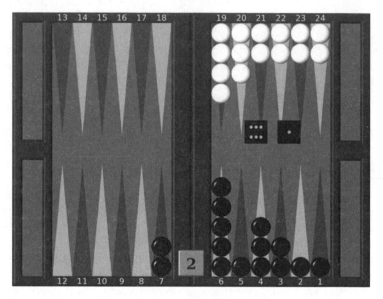

Bearing in. Black to play 6-1

It may seem automatic to play 7/6, 7/1 in this situation, bringing the last men in so Black can take two checkers off on his next roll. However, this decision fails to look ahead. Black will have two checkers on the ace point whatever play he makes. If he plays 7/6, 7/1, then on his second and subsequent 5s he will be forced to play 6/1 until he has cleared the 6-point. The result will be several checkers on the ace point, which will lead to later wastage. Instead, Black should play 7/1, 6/5, even though he will be able to bear off only one checker next roll. By putting a checker on the 5-point Black prepares to bear that checker off if he rolls a subsequent 5, thus reducing the number of dead checkers that end up on the ace point.

Tip 22

Rip Checkers Off

Once all your men are home and there is no contact with the opposition, you want to bear your checkers off as quickly and efficiently as possible. One very simple rule will solve a lot of your problems: if you have a checker on a point that corresponds to one of your dice, it is nearly always correct to use that die to take a checker off; in fact it has been proven that it is always correct to do so with a 1, 5 or 6. There are a few positions where actually it is not correct to bear a checker off with a 2, 3 or 4, even though you have a checker on the corresponding point, but these situations are so rare that they are not worth worrying about. Simply take a checker off. Even if you can use that part of the roll to unstack a heavy point; it is still correct to take the checker off. So if one of your dice is a 1 and you have a checker on the ace point, take that checker off the board, and then think about the other part of your roll.

However, if the numbers on both dice are needed to take a checker off, it may be better to use the roll to unstack heavy points and fill in empty points. For example:

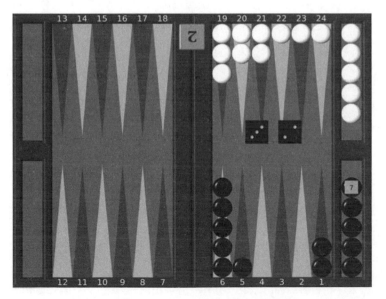

Bearing off (1). Black to play 3-2

Here, Black could take a man of with 5/0, but that is not the right play; however, this move would leave the 5- and 4-points empty. If Black then rolled a 5 or a 4, he would be forced to dump a checker onto the 2- or 1-point, and that would probably lead to extra wastage. Black is better off playing 6/4, 6/3, even though this does not take a checker off. Now Black can handle a 5 or a 4 without problem, and he will also have started to unstack the heavy 6-point.

Note that this move is correct only because Black needed to move from the stripped 5-point in order to be able to take a checker off. If Black had instead rolled 4-2, his correct play would have been 6/0 rather than 6/4, 6/2, the reason being that he clearly has to play 6/2 with the 4. This leaves him a 2 to play, and he has a checker on the 2-point. As we have seen, if you can use a die to take a checker off exactly, without losing pips, it is correct to do so.

The rules of the game specify that you must play both numbers of the dice if legally possible, but you are permitted to choose the order in which you play the numbers. As long as the play of a dice roll is legal at the point it is made, you may play either the smaller or larger number first. Taking advantage of this option can lead to some interesting strategies in the bear off.

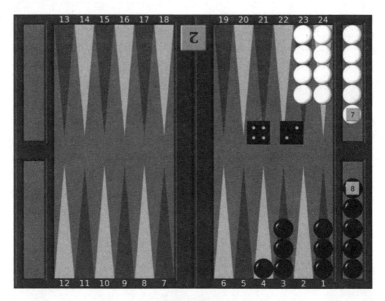

Bearing off (2). Black to play 4-2

In this example it may seem as though Black must play 4/0, 3/1 in order to play the roll legally. If he does that he will be unable to take two checkers off next turn if he rolls a 2, and that could cost him the game since he would then have five checkers left. Instead, Black should play 4/2, 3/0. This is quite legal. Black can choose to play the 2 first, and once he has done so then 3/0 is a legal play with the 4 since Black's highest point is the 3-point. Now if Black rolls a 2 next turn he will be able to take two checkers off.

If you are unable to take a checker off with part of your roll, it is generally correct to unstack heavy points and move checkers to unoccupied or thinly occupied points. This will diversify your checkers and maximize your chances of bearing a checker off with various rolls of the dice. It is seldom correct to stack checkers higher on a point in the hope of throwing a specific double. Instead, simply spread the checkers out and prepare for more dice rolls.

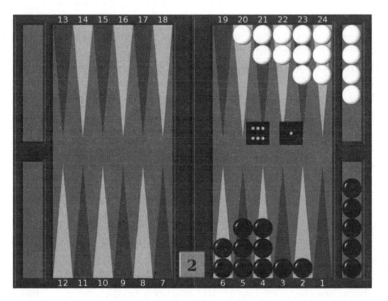

Bearing off (3). Black to play 6-1

Many players will play 6/0, 6/5 so that if they roll 5-5 on the next turn they will be able to take four checkers off. This is not correct. In the first place, if Black rolls a 6 next turn he will have to waste a pip, since with no checkers on the 6-point Black can only play 5 pips with the 6. Furthermore, Black's 3-point is thin. If Black plays 6/5 with the 1 and then rolls a few 3's before he can clear his 4 and 5-points, he will be forced to play those 3's to lower points causing eventual wastage. Black's proper play is 6/0, 4/3, spreading his checkers out so as to take full advantage of whatever he rolls.

Tip 23

Put Your Checkers Where They Belong

One of the features of backgammon is that your choices of move are restricted not only by the checkers on the board but also by the dice. You can play only what the dice will let you. For this reason, when you get a roll you are looking for it is important to take advantage of it immediately: if you are looking for a 5 and you roll a 5, it may be quite a while before another 5 appears.

Put your checkers where they belong. Do not fiddle around with something relatively unimportant. If you know you want a checker moved to a certain place, and you roll a number to move the checker there, do it. Of course you have to make an intelligent estimate of the priorities, and something else may crop up that is more important in the short run, but it is usually a good idea to make the move you know you will want to make.

As an example, suppose you have just one back checker that is behind a 5-prime and needs a 6 to escape. If you roll that 6, it is almost certainly correct to jump over the prime, regardless of what you might have been able to achieve elsewhere. Or if the back checker is not at the edge of the 5-prime but you roll the number needed to move to the edge, from where it can then escape with a 6, it is almost surely correct to move to the edge of the prime.

Another example would be when your opponent has escaped his back checkers and you are working on building a board to contain a checker that you hope to hit in the future. Suppose you have three checkers on your 3-point, and your 2-point is open. Where does that third checker on the 3-point belong? Not where it is, certainly. It is almost worthless there, and belongs on the 2-point where it will later be joined by another checker to make the point. So if you roll an ace and there is nothing else that needs dealing with, it is almost always correct to use the ace to move that third checker on the 3-point to where it belongs. This is even more valuable than, say, using that ace to slot your 5-point from a stack of checkers on the 6-point. The checkers on the 6-point have various places they might go; the checker on the 3-point has only one place it wants to be.

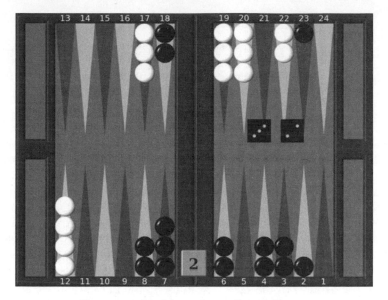

Put your checkers where they belong.
Black to play 3-2

On first glance 3-2 looks like the perfect roll for Black. It makes the 5-point, filling the gap in Black's board, so if Black later hits a shot he will be well placed to contain the hit checker.

Yes, 3-2 is indeed the perfect roll for Black, but not for that reason! Black needs to escape his back checker. The race is fairly close. Black's proper game plan is to get that back checker out to White's bar point. Then when Black rolls a number larger than 6, he can move that checker around. These moves will give Black time to maintain his strong board while waiting to hit a shot or roll doubles, and take the racing lead.

What happens if Black leaves the back checker where it is? Black might roll that needed 5 in the next few rolls, in which case it will not matter what he does now. But if Black does not roll that 5, he could be in trouble. He will not be able to move the back checker to safety, and he does not dare give up the anchor on White's bar point. That means that Black will be forced to absorb rolls with his front checkers, and soon he will be unable to do so without crunching his board. The back checker belongs on White's bar point, not on White's 2-point. Black has rolled the number to get it there, and that is what he must do.

Tip 24   Learn When to Take Risks and When to Play Safe

Backgammon is a game of risks and rewards. Unless the best move is obvious, your choice of move will inevitably offer some gains and some drawbacks. What you are trying to do is find the play that has maximal rewards and minimal risks for the given position.

A common example occurs when you are considering either slotting a key point or bringing down builders into your outer board. The rewards here are clear: when your opponent fails to hit you have a good chance to either make the slotted point or use the builders to make a good point. The risks are also clear: if you are hit you lose ground in the race, are stuck on the bar and suffer all the other bad things that happen when you get hit. The key is to determine when the rewards outweigh the risks, and vice versa. Here are some key criteria:

1) Strength of opponent's inner board
This is an important factor. If you are hit, you need to re-enter before you can regroup. If your opponent owns only his 6-point, it follows that you will have little difficulty re-entering. Each additional inner board point your opponent owns greatly increases the danger of flunking (see Glossary, page 138), or of being forced to re-enter awkwardly.

2) A defensive anchor
If your back checkers are anchored, you feel more secure about leaving blots on the offensive side of the board: if a blot is hit at least there will always be a place to enter and there is no need to worry about other checkers being battered about. If your back checkers are split, it is more dangerous to play boldly up front, since you might get hit in both places. A good rule of thumb is to avoid being weak on both sides of the board at the same time.

3) The race
If you are ahead in the race, getting hit is quite costly. You lose your racing lead and quite possibly go from being the favourite to the underdog. Conversely, if you are behind in the race, getting hit only puts you further behind, which is far less serious. You will need to

hit a shot or contain an enemy checker in any case. If you are behind, making new offensive points becomes more important in order to contain an enemy checker.

4) Number of men back
Every man you have back in your opponent's board has to be extricated. If you have zero or one checkers back, getting hit is quite serious. You were on your way towards running home safely, and now you have to start all over. If you have several checkers back, one more is not going to hurt much and may even be an asset.

5) Enemy checkers back
If your opponent has only one checker back, it is important to form a board as quickly as possible in order to blockade or attack that checker, or to keep it on the bar if you hit it as it tries to escape. If your opponent has several checkers back, forming an immediate board is less vital since not all of them will get out quickly.

6) Ease of playability otherwise
If not taking a chance forces you to make an extremely ugly and inflexible move, it is usually worth taking the risk of being hit rather than winding up with an unplayable position. If you can play the roll decently while playing safe, it is often correct to do so.

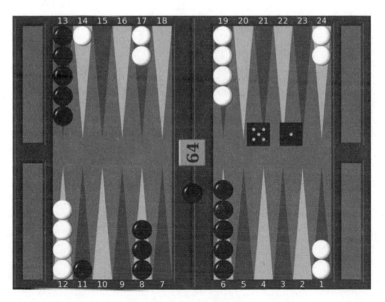

Bold vs. Safe (1). Black to play 5-1

It should be noted that these factors are also interdependent. The more men back you have relative to your opponent, the worse off you are in the race, and this argues for bold play. On the other hand, if he has more men back you are probably ahead in the race, arguing for safe play.

In the example above, Black is forced to enter with the 5. With the 1, he should play the relatively safe 11/10. He has only one checker back, White has the stronger inner board and is likely to attack the checker on his 5-point. Black does not want to give White another target to shoot at. Black's plan is to scramble his back checker around and win, without worrying about other distractions. By contrast:

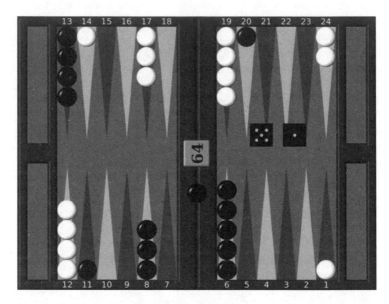

Bold vs. Safe (2). Black to play 5-1

This time Black should play boldly with b/20, 6/5. He has the solid anchor, so if he does get hit he will still have a playable game. Also Black has more men back than White and White is ahead in the race, so getting hit is not too painful for Black. And if White is unable to hit, then Black will be in great position to make his 5-point and put a lot of pressure on White's lone back checker. By contrast, 11/10 with ace would be too passive.

Tip 25   The Fastest Way to Make a Point is to Start It

In order to make a point, it is necessary to get two checkers on that point; since your choice of moves is restricted by what you roll on the dice, this is not always easy. Having varied builders aiming at the point is valuable, and each new builder greatly increases your chances of making the point. Still, that perfect roll may not appear.

It may be necessary to slot the point with one checker, hoping to cover it later. This is risky behaviour when your opponent has checkers back in your home board, since he may hit the slotted blot and cost you significant ground in the race. There are positions where such an aggressive slot is called for, but usually when your opponent has checkers back it is better to bring builders into your outer board, then try to make the point in one roll rather than leave a direct shot.

But it is another story if your opponent has escaped his back checkers. Now you can slot with safety – and you should, almost automatically, because the fastest way to make a point is to slot it. Once you have slotted the point, you need only one good number on the dice to make the point. You no longer need to wait for a perfect roll to make the point: you can do it in two rolls.

If you watch an expert play a holding game or an anchor game, it seems as though his board is almost always perfect when he finally gets his shot. An average player, on the other hand, may not be ready. The expert's secret is that once his opponent has escaped the back checkers he slots the points he needs as quickly as possible. As a result, he needs fewer good numbers to make the points.

What if your opponent may be leaving a shot on the next turn? Unless it is very likely that the shot will be coming exactly on the next turn, it is still correct to slot the point. You are going to need the point eventually in any event, so you may as well slot it now. If your opponent does leave the shot and you hit, it is not necessarily bad to have the key point slotted. If you are lucky, you might roll a perfect number to hit and cover. If not, maybe your opponent will not hit back from the bar, and then with the point slotted you will be a favourite to make the point on your next roll.

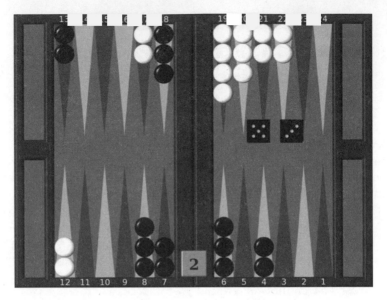

Starting a point. Black to play 5-3

Black could make his 3-point, but that would be a poor play. It is the 5-point that Black really needs, since filling in that gap gives him a solid blockade to contain a hit checker. If the 5-point is open, White will always be one roll away from escaping. Making the 3-point costs Black vital builders for the 5-point. In addition, if Black is unable to move the spare on White's bar point safely next turn, Black will be forced into giving up one of his points.

In this situation 18/10 looks reasonable, bringing in a new builder for the 5-point. Black could then go on to make his 5-point next turn with any combination of 1s, 2s, 3s and 5s. But Black can do better: the proper play is 18/13, 8/5, starting the 5-point. Now all Black needs is a 1, 2 or 3 on one of his die to make the 5-point. In addition, if Black rolls any 1, or two dice totalling 8, he can make his 5-point and retain a solid 5-prime. Thus, by slotting the point Black leaves himself more rolls to make the point next turn. It is true that if White rolls specifically 6-1 next roll he will be forced to leave a shot while the 5-point is slotted. But that does not matter – the probability of it happening is low, and even if it does Black maybe will hit and cover. Black absolutely must have his 5-point for the upcoming rolls, when White gets squeezed off the midpoint, and starting the 5-point is the fastest way to make it.

Tip 26   Avoid Ugly Plays

Anybody can play a good roll well; the true test of skill is how you handle a bad roll. When the dice fail to cooperate and the checkers can only go to inferior places, it becomes important to make the best of a bad situation.

Sometimes it might seem as though there just is no playable move. When that seems to be the case, many players just shove the checkers onto awful places and, as a result, their game deteriorates to the point where it is unrecoverable. Avoid doing this: if a move looks so ugly that you feel sick, do not make it. Look around hard for some other move. Avoid the really ugly plays, even if perhaps you will have to leave a shot or break a point you would rather hold.

It is true that sometimes you just have no choice. You really cannot afford to leave a shot when your opponent has a very strong board. Some points are simply impossible to break. But do try to avoid the ugly play if at all possible. Look hard, and very often a move you normally would not have considered suddenly becomes a pretty play compared to the ugly alternative.

Here are three ugly plays to avoid:

1) Going deep in the inner board.
2) Piling extra checkers onto useless places, from which you will be unable to move them conveniently.
3) Getting stuck in enemy territory behind a blockade.

Even an intermediate player has a feel for what does and does not look nice. It if looks ugly, it is. Find something else.

The example on page 72 shows a poor roll for Black. He cannot afford to move a back checker, since that would leave him too exposed to being attacked, so the 6 must come from the midpoint. The safe play is 13/2 — but that is so, so ugly. It is not just that it goes behind White's anchor and deep into the board –Black could live with that. What really hurts is piling that third checker onto the 2-point, where it might just as well be out of play. Even though getting hit would be very bad, Black is better off playing 13/8, 13/7. This strategy keeps Black's checkers in play and puts them on decent points. On the bright side, if White misses the shot then

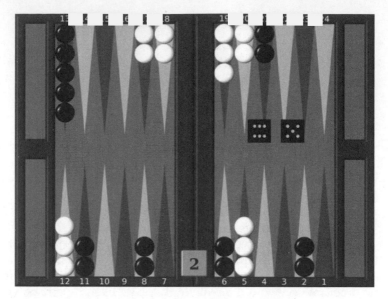

Avoiding ugly play (1). Black to play 6-5

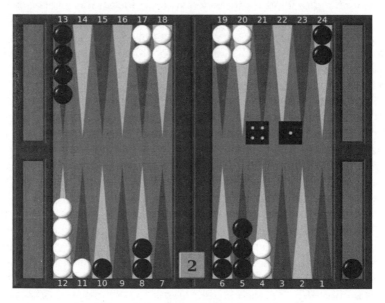

Avoiding ugly play (2). Black to play 4-1

Black will have a good chance to cover the blot on the bar point and improve his blockade. And 13/8, 13/7 is so much prettier than 13/2 that it just has to be right.

Black could play safe with b/24, 10/6, which brings the outfield checker to an optimal place. But this play would leave three checkers on White's ace point – very ugly! Those checkers are hemmed in; White already has a solid 4-prime, and if Black plays b/24, 10/6 White will be free to bring some more ammunition down and threaten to extend the blockade. Black will soon be hemmed in with nowhere to go. The proper play is b/21, 24/23, which is much prettier. This spreads out the back checkers before they get hemmed in and gives Black excellent opportunities to make an anchor on White's 4-point, after which Black will have a reasonable game. There is little danger in temporarily having no anchor in White's board, since White has no attack ammunition in place. Black would rather not leave the direct shot on his 10-point, of course, but his clear priority is to untangle the mess on White's side of the board.

Tip 27 Learn Doubling Cube Basics

One of the first questions people ask about backgammon is, 'so what's that funny block with all the numbers on it for?' That 'funny block' is the doubling cube, and it adds a significant degree of interest and skill to the game of backgammon: in the hands of a skilled player, it is a very powerful weapon. Learning how to use the doubling cube is easy; mastering the nuances requires a great deal of practice and study.

At the beginning of each game, the cube starts out in the middle of the board. It is typically turned so that the number 64 faces upwards, although this is not strictly necessary. When the cube is in the centre, each game has a value of one point. When the cube is in the centre, either player may offer a double on their turn. They do this by turning the cube to 2, placing it on their opponent's side of the board, and saying, 'I double'. This must be done at the start of the player's turn, *before* he rolls the dice.

The doubler's opponent has two options at this point: he can accept the cube, or reject it. If the opponent rejects the double, he loses one point, the cube is placed back in the centre of the board and the game is over. If he accepts, the cube is placed on his side of the board (typically in the checker storage tray, or on the table next to the board) and the doubler rolls the dice. The game is now being played for two points.

Once the cube has been turned and accepted, it is 'owned' by the player who accepted the double – he now has exclusive rights to double again. Should the game turn around so that he is now leading, he can double when it is his turn (before he rolls the dice). He does this by turning the cube to 4, placing it in front of his opponent and saying, 'I double'. At this point his opponent can then accept the cube and play on for four points, or he can reject the cube and lose two points. If he accepts, he has exclusive control of the cube. This doubling process can continue indefinitely, though it is very rare for the doubling cube to go past the 8.

So when should you double? When should you accept or drop? Entire books have been written on this subject but, in general, you should double when you are a firm favourite to win the game, but not such a favourite that you are likely to win a gammon or backgammon. (This does not apply if the Jacoby rule is being used – see tip 15.) If you have a good chance of winning a gammon, it is usually better to play on and try to win two points, rather than doubling and letting your opponent escape for just one.

When should you take, or agree to double? The basic rule of thumb is that you should take the cube when you have about a 25 per cent chance of winning the game, ignoring gammons and backgammons. If there is a good chance that if you lose the game you will be gammoned, then you should have higher chances of winning, to compensate for this.

But, unfortunately, backgammon boards do not come equipped with magic genies to tell you precisely what your winning chances are. With experience, you will start to get a feel for how good or bad your position is. But, until then, here is a simpler strategy: double when you think that you are comfortably ahead in the game. Accept the cube if you can see a clear strategy for turning the game around, and that strategy only requires a moderate amount of luck.

Tip 28

Every Roll is a New Cube Decision

Your opponent has just rolled the dice. He makes his move and picks up his dice. It is your turn. You grab your dice cup, shake the dice and roll them, anxious to see what your next roll will be. If the cube is in the centre, or if you own the cube, you have just committed one of the most common errors of backgammon: you have failed to consider doubling. It is easy to get caught up in the excitement of the game and forget about the cube. Backgammon is a thrilling game with a lot of twists and turns, and there is a natural impulse to quickly roll the dice and see what happens. Try to control that impulse. Before you roll the dice, the first part of every play should be a conscious decision on whether or not to double. Try to get into the habit of thinking about the cube before every roll.

For most of the time, the decision about doubling will be trivial. For instance, if you are an underdog in the game or only a slight favourite, then it will obvious that you should not double. But failing to double when you should have can be very costly. If you roll very well it will be easy for your opponent to pass on doubling next turn, while he might otherwise have taken the opportunity to double; you will win only one point instead of two (or four, if you would have won a gammon). On the other hand, if your opponent would have passed the double in any case, you still give him a free shot to roll a good number and get back into the game, when you could have locked up a certain point. Either way, missing out on a doubling opportunity by not thinking about the cube could lose you the game.

It is never too early to think about doubling. For example, suppose your opponent wins the opening roll and rolls 5-4, playing 24/20, 13/8. You roll a great 3-3, playing 8/5(2)*, 6/3(2). Your opponent rolls 6-6, staying on the bar. You're excited. The game has only just begun, and you've already made two new points in your home board. Your opponent is on the bar, and you have builders in place to make another point. You, as Black, now roll:

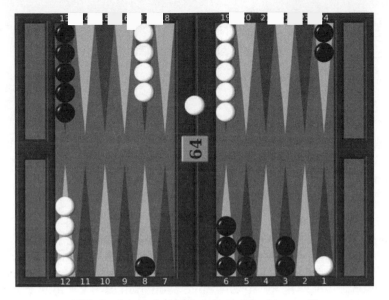

Think about doubling first. Black on roll

Wait, don't roll those dice – turn the cube! In this example, Black has a substantial advantage even though it is only his second roll of the game: he has two new inner board points, White is on the bar and White is also quite undeveloped. Should White take (accept the double)? Well, really that is White's problem. If White passes on the double then Black collects an immediate point, one he might not win if he fails to double and White rolls well on the next turn. If White takes, Black might roll another great number, such as 6-6; after that, White would definitely pass and Black would lose his opportunity to win more than one point. But if Black simply rolls the dice without thinking about doubling he loses the opportunity to cash in on his good first roll.

Tip 29

The Doubling Cup is Half Full

Often a player with the advantage will be considering turning the cube, but will then start thinking of all the bad things that might happen. He sees bad rolls that will leave a shot, opportunities for his opponent to make new points, opposing primes closing in on him, and other backgammon nightmares. By the time his position improves to the point where these 'bad things' are very unlikely to happen, his opponent will have a clear pass. Meanwhile, the nervous player will have lost the opportunity to double, when he could have put the pressure on with a cube that might have induced a premature pass, or might have won him two or four points instead of only one.

There is plenty of luck in backgammon. Unless you have an overwhelming lead in a straight race, there is always something 'bad' that can happen. There are usually plenty of good things on the horizon as well, and these improvements are often far more likely than the ugly outcomes you dread. You must not let fear of the nightmare scenario prevent you from turning the cube – instead, be an optimist, seeing the cup as half full rather than half empty. Look for the good things that can happen – all the things that would make you regret *not* turning the cube.

Of course the bad thing may happen and you will lose two points as a result of choosing to double. But you just need to accept this pragmatically, keeping in mind that it was the lousy dice that cost the game, not your decision to turn the cube. You would probably have lost the game even if you had not doubled, although you have lost two points instead of one. But then again, if things do go badly, doubling only costs you that one extra point compared to what might have transpired if you had not doubled.

In backgammon as in life, fear can prevent you from taking full advantage of a good situation. Don't let a few unlikely possibilities scare you into sitting on the cube – if things are mostly favourable, send the cube over.

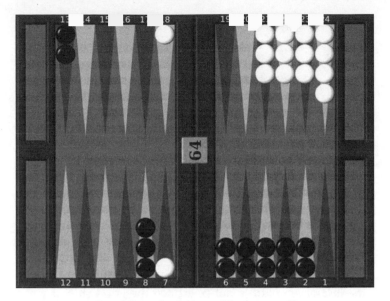

Doubling decisions. Black on roll

White had been sitting on Black's bar point hoping to roll doubles, but in fact never rolled them and finally got squeezed off the bar point. Black may be worrying about what will happen if he misses – White will then be miles ahead in the race and he will almost certainly lose. Black might consider it better make that hit first, before going on to turn the cube.

Yet this is not the proper way of thinking. Consider the probabilities of Black hitting: he does this with all 1s, all 6s, 2-2, 3-3 and 4-2. That comes to 24 of his 36 possible rolls. And if Black does hit, he will be an overwhelming favourite to win the game, with White on the bar against Black's strong board. *Now* is the time to double, rather than after hitting the shot. If Black waits, White will have a clear pass if the shot is hit, so Black must turn the cube now to collect his two points if he hits. Black must look on the bright, rather than the dark side: he is a clear favourite to hit and win, so he should double.

Tip 30   The Taking Cup is Half Full

When your opponent turns the cube, it is because you are at a disadvantage. It is very tempting to decide not to take the cube, reckoning that if you are losing the game you should not risk losing two points. But it is not that simple, and if you think that way you will pass just about all doubles.

The key to this conundrum is that, while you do lose two points in total if you take the double and lose the game, in reality you only risk losing one point. Think about it: if you pass the double you will lose out on one point in any case, so by taking the double you only risk the loss of one additional point. On the good side, if you take and win the game, you win two points. But actually you will have won three points, since you will be winning two points instead of *losing* the one point you would have lost by passing the double. Thus, if you take the double you are risking one point in order, potentially, to gain three points. This means that you can afford to take, even when you are the underdog, since on balance passing is more costly. If you can win the game more than 25 per cent of the time, you will do better to take than to pass.

Gammons come into play in making cube decisions. There is often the possibility that you will be gammoned, in which case you will lose four points (or, in reality, three additional points) rather than two points (or one additional point). If there is a significant chance that you will be gammoned, you need better winning chances to justify taking the double.

But on the other hand, if you take the double you own something your opponent does not – the cube. Now he has to play the game to conclusion in order to win, since he cannot double you again. If the game turns around, however, you alone have the option of redoubling. If you redouble and your opponent has to pass, you will not have to play the game to conclusion and risk another turnaround. When you own the cube, you will sometimes be able to redouble later and force your opponent to drop. Because owning the cube conveys this additional value, you can take with slightly less than a 25 per cent winning chance. Put this thinking into practice. When you are doubled, do not think of all the bad things that might happen. After all, they will always be out there since – unless your opponent has made a terrible double – you are currently the underdog. So be an optimist and think of all the good things that might happen: if there are a sufficient number of them, you have a take.

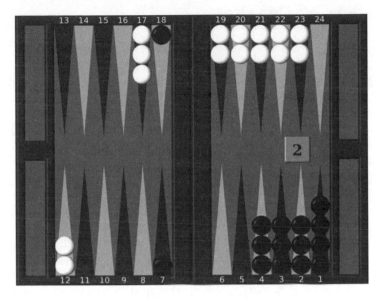

White doubles. Does Black take?

It is would be easy for Black to reason that White is a favourite to hit and, if he does, Black has almost no chance. Even if White does not hit, there is still no guarantee of getting by, so it would be best to pass the double. That is the wrong attitude to adopt if you are adopting the requisite 'cup half full' attitude. You might instead reason that White misses on fully 1/3 of his rolls. If White does miss, Black is miles ahead in the race. It is true that Black might not escape, but this is where cube ownership comes into play. If White does miss then Black can redouble and, with the race so lopsided, it is probable that White will be unable to even take. In addition, there is virtually no gammon danger, since Black has most of his men home. Therefore Black will win 1/3 of the time when White misses, as well as occasionally when White hits. These are definitely higher than 25 per cent winning odds, so Black should take the cube.

Tip 31   Don't Lose Your Market

Suppose you have a strong position with a great deal of potential for big improvement on the next exchange of rolls – if you roll well and/or if your opponent rolls badly. If you were to double now, he would have a clear take. You choose not to double and you do make a big improvement on the next exchange of rolls. Now you double, and he properly passes.

So, consider how you feel about this turn of events. If you are happy to have collected a sure point, you do not have the right attitude. Your thinking should properly focus on why you failed to double the previous roll. Because if you had doubled the previous roll, your opponent would have taken, and you would have had a good chance to win two points (or four points, if you had gone on to win a gammon). But, instead, you won a measly one point when you doubled and he passed. While it would still be possible to lose the game, of course, on balance you would have done better by doubling earlier, if he now has a pass. By waiting too long you have lost your market.

When you have an advantage and the position is very volatile, it is tempting to think 'let's take a roll and see which way the wind is blowing before turning the cube'. This is not a winner's way of thinking: if you wait, there is too much danger that you will make big gains on the next exchange and you will then lose your market, by a great deal – an expensive result. Certainly it is true that things may go badly on the next exchange and your advantage will disappear, but that simply means that you are playing for twice the stakes now, with perhaps only a slight advantage. And you can still win the game.

If the position is not very volatile, then it is usually correct to hold off doubling if your opponent has a clear take. Even if things go well on the next exchange, he will still probably have a take, or close to it. So you will have no great regrets if your position improves, you double next roll – and he passes. In this type of situation you have more to lose than gain by doubling.

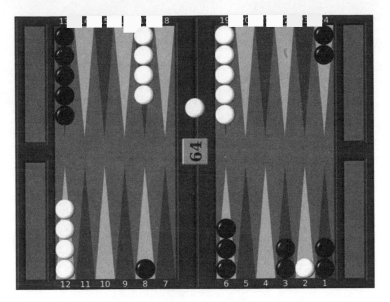

Losing the market (1). Black on roll

This position occurs after White wins the opening roll with 5-1 and plays 24/23, 13/8, Black rolls 5-5 and makes his 3- and 1-points, and White flunks (see Glossary entry, 'dance'). Clearly Black has the advantage here, with his racing lead, stronger inner board and White being on the bar. But White still has an easy take if Black doubles. The game is young, and Black is short on ammunition to follow through with an attack – and if White gets an anchor in Black's board the game will be close to even. Yet Black should definitely double in this situation. This position is very volatile because while Black has a few crushing rolls, more important is what White does next turn. Most likely Black will bring some builders down from the midpoint, preparing to attack. If White enters with a 2, or rolls something like 5-3 to make Black's 5-point, then White will be in fine shape. But if White should happen to flunk again, Black will have a very big advantage – and if he then doubles, White will have a clear pass. So Black cannot afford to wait and see what happens. Instead, he must double now and not risk losing his market.

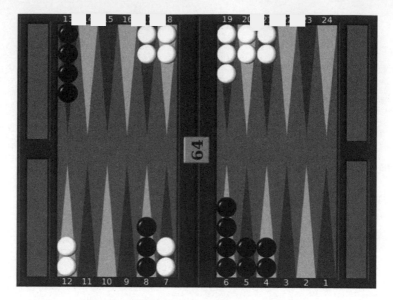

Losing the market (2). Black on roll

In this case, Black has a clear advantage. He is up ten pips in the race and has the more advanced anchor. If Black doubled, White would have a trivial take with both decent racing chances and the chance of hitting a shot when Black gets squeezed off the midpoint. Black should not double in this very volatile position. Black will only lose his market if he rolls doubles other than 1-1 or 6-6, while if it is White who rolls the doubles the game becomes an even race. Most of the time nothing much happens, and White will still have a take on the next roll, so Black should just roll and see what happens. On the one hand, if Black gains more in the race then he will have a decent double, but White will still have a take. But, on the other, if Black loses ground in the race then he will be happy he chose not to double.

Tip 32

If it Might Be a Pass, Double

Many players are unsure of themselves when it comes to turning the cube. They know that they need an advantage, but are not sure how much of an advantage is required. In consequence they often wait too long to double and fail to collect the extra points they could have won had they doubled when their opponent still had a take.

In order to determine whether or not to double, it is necessary to see how things look from the other side of the table. Put yourself in your opponent's shoes and ask yourself, 'if I were doubled in his position, would I take?' It might seem that there are only two possible answers to this question, but in fact there are three:

1) Yes, I would definitely take
2) No, I would definitely pass
3) I'm not sure

Your choice of answer will usually determine whether or not you should double. If the answer is 'I'm not sure', then it is always correct to double. It may seem odd that the more unsure you are about the position, the more sure you are that turning the cube is correct. Yet this is the proper strategy, for the following reasons:

1) Your opponent might pass.
If you are not sure whether or not it is a take, he will not be either. If he would be passing the double, it is clearly better to double rather than give your opponent a free shot to get back in the game.

2) Your opponent might take when he should have passed.
Since you are not sure whether or not he should take, maybe he is supposed to pass, but will not. If this happens you have caused him to make an error by doubling, and if things go well you will win extra points.

3) Even if your opponent should take and properly does so, turning the cube cannot be far wrong, if it is wrong at all. You thought it might possibly be a pass, you must definitely have the advantage in the game. Since turning the cube amounts to doubling the stakes of

the game, it cannot be a bad thing for this to happen when you have the advantage.

So remember, if you are not sure whether or not your opponent will take, then you should *always* double – with no exceptions. This maximizes your profits when your opponent takes and you win, and gives him the opportunity to make a mistake by taking when he should pass, or by passing when he should take.

If the answer to 'if I were doubled in his position, would I take?' is definitely a 'yes', then it is usually wrong to double, even if you have the advantage. The reason is that your advantage is evidently small; if things go well on the next turn you can double and he will still have a take, so you will not have lost anything by waiting. It is possible that the position is so volatile that you may be crushing him with a good roll, in which case it could be right to double and hope you roll well.

If the answer to the question is definitely 'no', then it is usually right to double. The only reason not to double would be that your position is so strong that you prefer to play on for a gammon. Most of the time, the best option is to turn the cube and take the almost-guaranteed win. In addition, he might make the mistake of taking, and that would certainly be to your advantage.

Tip 33   Be Slower to Double When You Own the Cube

At the start of the game, the cube is in the centre, equally available to both players, so there is nothing you can do to prevent your opponent from doubling if he so desires. Whether you double him or not, he will still have the option of doubling you. Doubling now costs you the option of doubling later, but it does not have any effect on your opponent's doubling options.

If you already own the cube, the story's different, because so long as you retain possession of the cube, your opponent does not have the option of doubling. Once you choose to redouble, things change: not only do you lose the option of doubling later; you also give your opponent the option of doubling, which he would not have had if you had kept the cube.

Since cube ownership is valuable, you need to be a bit more cautious with your redoubles than was necessary for your initial doubles, when the cube was in the centre. If things go well, whether you owned the cube or not will make no difference – you will win twice the amount if you double. But if things go badly there *will* be a difference that depends on whether you owned the cube and redoubled, or if this was an initial doubling. If the cube is in the centre you would be facing a possible double from your opponent whether you had doubled or not. However, if you own the cube and hold off doubling, you will not have to face the chance of a recube. Instead, you will be able to play the game until the end, without having to pay more.

Yet it is important not to become too cautious, just because you own the cube. If you have a solid double, go ahead and make it – regardless of cube location. Remember that the object of doubling is to double the stakes when you have the advantage; this works whether the cube is in the centre or in your possession. It is the marginal doubles that are easy takes that you should avoid making when you own the cube.

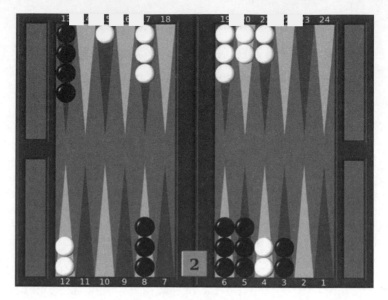

Ownership (1). Black on roll

With the cube in the centre Black has a reasonable double, although White has an easy take. Black is ahead 23 pips in the race, which is a pretty good lead, and he has several rolls that can improve his position, a couple of which will give his opponent a clear pass. White has good odds, of hitting a shot and also of winning the race, that are easily good enough to justify taking.

If Black owns the cube, however, he should hold off doubling. The double is marginal in any case, since not a lot is likely to happen on the next roll. But in the possible outcomes where White either hits a shot or pulls ahead in the race, Black will dearly regret having redoubled; if White then has access to the cube, he would be likely to have a powerful redouble. But if the cube is in the centre, then Black cannot prevent White from doubling. In this case the above argument for holding off no longer exists.

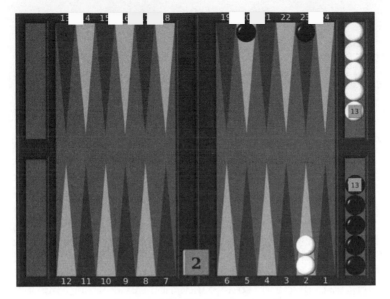

Ownership (2). Black on roll

Here, of the 36 possible rolls available, 19 rolls get Black off, and that makes Black the favourite. If the cube is in the centre, Black should double. He is the favourite and will not get another chance to double, so he must strike while the iron is hot. Of course if Black fails to get off, White will redouble, since White gets off the board on 26 of the available 36 rolls (and in this case Black should take, since he is the underdog, with odds of less than 3 to 1). But there is nothing Black can do to prevent this situation arising: with the cube in the centre, White has cube access whether or not Black doubles.

The situation changes dramatically if Black owns the cube. Now, by not doubling, Black forfeits his slight 19-17 advantage, but shows a big gain from not having to face White's powerful redouble if he fails to get off. Preventing this redouble is very important, so Black should hold on to the cube.

It is interesting to note that if White's two checkers were on the ace point rather than the 2-point, Black should redouble even if he owns the cube. The reason is that, in this case, allowing White cube access no longer matters – if Black fails to get off, then White automatically wins. Therefore, since Black is the favourite he should just go ahead and up the stakes.

Tip 34   Know When to Play On for a Gammon

When you have a big advantage in the game, it is usually correct to turn the cube. You do not mind if your opponent passes – that is a certain point for you – but neither do you mind if he takes, because then you have a chance to win two points, or four points if you win a gammon. Failing to double under such circumstances merely gives your opponent a chance to roll a lucky number that will get him back in the game, without having to pay for the opportunity to roll that number.

Occasionally you may roll such an opportune number that your chances swing from so-so to a near lock in that one roll. If you go on to double after that stroke of good fortune, your opponent will pass and you will only win the value of the cube. In this situation it may be better not to double but just to roll on, hoping to win a gammon.

Note that for money play the normal assumption is that undoubled gammons do not count, so if the cube is in the centre there is no point in waiting – just double and get on to the next game. Only if you own the cube might it be profitable to wait when you have a big advantage. If you are playing a match in a tournament there is no such restriction and undoubled gammons do count, so even with the cube in the centre it may be right to wait.

If you are considering playing on for a gammon as opposed to doubling, there are three things to consider:

1) If you were to double, is it absolutely certain that your opponent has a pass, and is it absolutely certain that he *will* pass?
This is most important. If there is any realistic chance that he would or should *take* your double, then you should always turn the cube. There is always the possibility that he might take and you then gammon him for twice the amount.

2) How good are your gammon odds?
If your odds of getting a gammon are non-existent, there is no point in playing on, risking the possibility that something bad will happen. If you do have some chance of getting a gammon, it may be worth taking the risk.

3) What is the danger of a turnaround?
If it is very unlikely that your opponent can win the game, you can afford to play on even with relatively small gammon chances. But if there is a significant danger that the game may turn against you, then you need good odds of getting a gammon to make it worth the risk of playing on.

Assuming your opponent is in such bad shape that he must pass, you must weight your odds of getting a gammon against the possibility of a turnaround in the game. This is often a difficult judgement, but keep in mind that you are risking twice as much as you stand to gain. To illustrate this, suppose you own the cube at 2 and are certain that if you redouble to 4 your opponent should, and would, pass. If you play on and are right, you gain two points, since you win four points when you would have won only two points had you redoubled. If you play on and win a single game, you win two points. If you play on and win a gammon, you win four points total or two extra points. However, if you play on and lose the game then you lose four points – the two that you would have won if you'd doubled and your opponent passed, plus the two that your opponent gains. By playing on for a gammon, you take the risk of losing four points for the possible reward of winning two extra points. Another important point to keep in mind is that your decision to play on for the gammon is not a commitment to do so for the rest of the game. Every time it is your roll it is vital to re-assess the situation and make a conscious decision on whether or not to double and cash the guaranteed point or to continue to play on. Once again, every roll is a new cube decision, and the decision on whether or not to double must be made at every turn.

Since if you choose to play on you will have the option of doubling next roll, you do not need to worry about your opponent creeping back into the game. Assuming you are alert, if things start to go badly you will be able to double at some point later and he will still have to pass. It is the instant turnaround that you have to fear. As long as there is little or no danger of such a sharp turnaround that your opponent will suddenly have a take, you can continue to play on. You have a free chance to win a gammon. If you choose to play on you will still have the option of doubling next roll. Therefore, you do not need to worry about your opponent gradually creeping back into the game – if you are alert to this you will be able to double and force him to pass. The bigger threat is an instant turnaround, where one roll can improve his chances dramatically. If there is little to no danger of such a sharp turnaround, then you can continue to play on for the gammon.

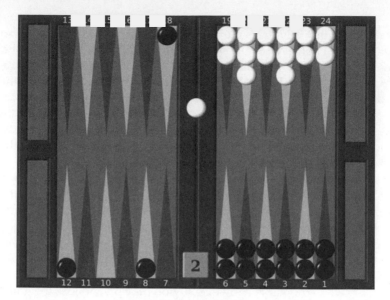

Playing on (1). Black on roll

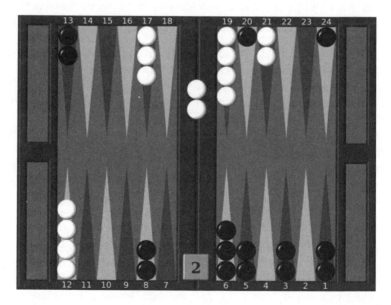

Playing on (2). Black on roll

In the top example on the opposite page, White has all his men but one home, so it is very unlikely that Black will win a gammon. Black could still lose the game, either if he is forced to leave a shot that White hits or if White gets very lucky in the race. Despite this, it is 100 per cent clear that Black should play on. Whatever he rolls next turn he will not leave a shot, and after he sees how things look next turn, he can re-evaluate. If there is danger of leaving a shot on the next roll, or if White enters and threatens to get back in the race, Black can always choose to double before White has a chance to carry out the threat.

In the bottom example, if Black doubles then White has a very clear pass, with two checkers on the bar against a four point board, so there is danger in playing on for the gammon. If White rolls 2-2 or 4-4 from the bar he will be right back in the game, and Black will no longer be able to claim a guaranteed point. Still, Black's gammon chances are quite good, so it is worth playing on and taking this risk.

Tip 35   Double Volatile Positions

Volatility is a measure of how much of a swing is likely to occur on the next exchange of rolls. If something exciting is likely to happen on the next exchange, the position is volatile, but if things are likely to stay fairly much the same, the position is considered involatile.

A good example of an involatile position is a holding game where both sides have spare checkers to play with. Nothing much is likely to happen and neither player is going to leave a shot in the near future. Certainly somebody might roll big doubles and change the race, but the probability of that happening is low. Another example of an involatile situation is a back game in its formative stages. Little is likely to happen on one exchange: the defensive checkers will still be there and the timing probably will not change too much on one roll.

An example of a volatile position is a blitz. Here there may be a big swing in the direction of the game if a second checker is hit, or if the player getting blitzed does or does not enter immediately. Another example is when a player is shooting at a key shot, where hitting the shot will probably produce a win, or even a gammon, while missing the shot will make him an underdog. In this case there is a lot riding on whether he hits the shot.

How does volatility affect a decision on whether or not to double? Many players are afraid to double when they have a good advantage in a volatile position. They prefer to take a roll and see what happens, reckoning that if things go well then they will double, while if things go badly they will be happy they chose not to. The problem with this approach is that, due to the volatility of the position, if things go well they go *very* well, and now their opponent will have an easy decision – pass. It is vital to double the volatile position, forcing your opponent to pay to see what happens.

Conversely, in an involatile position players are more willing to double since they know the game will not turn around in one roll. But once again, this is the wrong philosophy. Assuming your opponent has a clear take now, the involatility of the position means that he will almost certainly have a take next turn as well, since you are not likely to improve much. This time it is correct to wait and see what happens, since it does not cost you anything to do so. If you improve you can double next turn and he will still be taking, while if you get worse you will be happy you chose not to double.

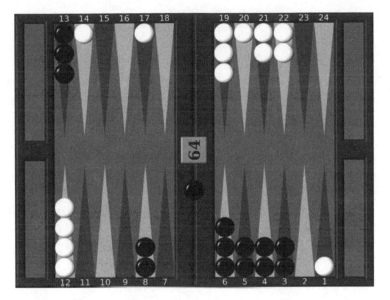

Volatile positions. Black on roll

Should Black double here? Black hits a shot with 17 numbers (any 5, 1-4, 2-3 and 2-6). If Black hits, he is in a great position. White will almost certainly have a clear pass after being hit. On the other hand, if Black flunks he is in serious trouble. White is very likely to cover the blot on the 5-point, and then White will be the favourite since Black is on the bar. Despite the risks, Black should double. He hits with 17 rolls and flunks with only 9 rolls, so the odds are well in his favour. The volatility is huge and Black has the advantage, so this is a perfect time to turn the cube. Waiting costs too much in the case where Black does go on to hit a shot.

Tip 36   Look for Alternate Ways to Win

When you are doubled, you need to look for ways to win in order to justify taking. The more ways to win you have, the better your winning odds. For example, suppose you are behind in a straight race with no further contact and you are doubled. There is only one way to win: you have to out-roll your opponent. Of course that does not necessarily mean you have to pass. If your racing odds are good enough to get you over the 25 per cent mark, you can take. But you can only win on the race.

In a more complex position, there are often several possible ways to win. While any one of these ways may have low probability, when all are combined they may add up to more than the 25 per cent needed to win the game.

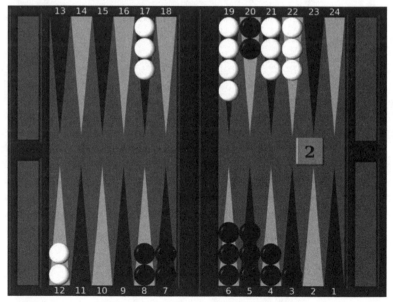

White doubles – does Black take?

In this example, Black has three ways that he can win the game. Firstly, he can hit an indirect 8-shot when White clears the midpoint. Unless White rolls doubles soon, White will eventually have to leave that indirect shot exposed. Secondly, he can hit a direct shot when White tries to clear the 8-point or the 6-point. Thirdly, he can win the race.

None of these possibilities has a very high probability of happening. Even if White leaves the indirect shot, which he might not, Black hits it with only 6 out of his 36 rolls. White would have to roll a very unlucky number to leave a direct shot – 6-3 or 6-1 when clearing the 8-point, and 6-1 or 5-1 when clearing the 6-point. Black is 19 pips behind in the race, which is a fairly substantial amount. None of these possibilities on its own would be sufficiently likely to justify taking the risk. But add them all together and Black has enough winning chances to take the cube. There are two important considerations: one is that Black is very unlikely to get gammoned, and the other is that Black's board is very strong, and likely to remain so for several rolls – so if Black does hit a shot it will probably be a winning one.

It should be noted that while Black has several different ways to win, he will not necessarily be able to capitalize on all of them simultaneously. For example, if Black rolls an early 6-6 the race will be about even, but Black will be running so he will not be hitting a shot. Conversely, if Black rolls small numbers he maximizes his chances of both hitting a shot and retaining a strong board to contain the hit checker, but his racing chances go down the drain. Still, the different ways for Black to turn the game around add up to enough winning chances for Black to take the cube.

It is impossible for us mere mortals to actually calculate these complicated odds – we just have to use experience and gut instinct.

Tip 37

Learn Match Play Basics

In normal backgammon, sometimes called 'money play' even when no money is on the line, each game is scored separately. You may agree ahead of time that you will play for a certain length of time or until one of you is tired of playing, and at the end you tally up the score and see who won for the day, and by how much. If you are playing for actual money you will settle up, based on the difference between your scores.

In match play, however, you agree to play until a player reaches a certain number of points, and then that person will be the winner of the match. Matches are almost always for an odd number of points. It does not matter what the final score is – in a 7-point match, a score of 7-6 is just as good as 7-0.

In match play, a special rule called the Crawford rule is generally used. The Crawford rule says that when someone reaches one point away from winning the match, the doubling cube may not be used in the next game. After that game has finished it is permissible for the trailer to double. Technically it is okay for the leading player to double as well, but since at this stage he has nothing to gain and everything to lose by doing so, this would be a very serious mistake.

Here is a practical illustration of how the Crawford rule works: Bob and Joe are playing a match to 9 points. After several games, Bob wins a game and brings the score to 8-3, in his favour. During the very next game, the cube is out of play. If Bob wins that game (called the Crawford game), the match is over, but if Joe wins the game, the score becomes 8-4 and Joe may double in any subsequent game. In fact, Joe should always double at his first opportunity, since it effectively costs him nothing to do so.

See tip 40 for some subtle but important strategy adjustments that are introduced when using the Crawford rule.

Tip 38   Understand Match Strategy

There can be quite a large difference between strategies in money play and match play. In money play, each point you win is a point your opponent loses, so every point is equal. In a match, you only win points; the first player to reach a specified number of points wins the match. Consequently, in match play your cube decisions – and sometimes your checker play – must be geared to aiming for that number of points, rather than winning the most points possible.

One obvious feature in match play strategy is as follows: Suppose your opponent turns the cube to a level such that if you accept and then lose the game you lose the match. For example, if you are behind 9-5 in an 11-point match and he doubles to 2. If you do choose to accept in this situation, it is vital that you redouble immediately, because you have everything to gain and nothing to lose. This may seem trivial, but there have been several instances in important tournaments where a player has forgotten to make this automatic redouble and it has cost him the match.

When you are ahead in the match you have less need for extra points than your opponent, particularly if any extra points you might gain will put your score higher than the number of points you need to win the match. Therefore, as the leader in the match you should be more conservative than normal with the cube, both on doubling and on taking. This is especially true if a redouble to 4 or higher is involved, or if there is a reasonable chance that somebody might win a gammon. Here, you do not need the extra points, but your opponent does.

Conversely, if you are behind in the match you should be more aggressive than normal with the cube, both with your doubles and with your takes. A higher cube gives you the chance to win quite a few points and get back into the match. Of course you still want to have some advantage when you double and you still need some chance of winning to justify a take, but you can be very liberal with your doubles and takes.

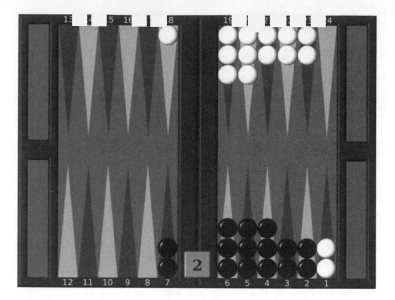

Black ahead 8-3 in 11-point match.
Black on roll, owning 2-cube

In money play, White would have a trivial pass if Black redoubled to 4. White's odds of winning are not nearly good enough to justify a take. At the match score, however, it is an entirely different situation. If White passes he will be behind 10-3 with very small odds of winning the match. White would be much better off taking and then, of course, immediately redoubling to 8, since he would have everything to gain and nothing to lose. Then if White does win the game he would win the match, and his chances of winning the game are much better than his chances of winning the match behind 10-3. In fact, it would be a big blunder for Black to redouble and give White this opportunity. So Black should sit on that cube and be happy to win without redoubling, and be ahead 10-3. In addition Black might win a gammon, and then he will win the match outright without needing to redouble.

Checker play can be different in matches depending on the match score. The deciding factor may be gammons. If your score is such that you only need to win the game to win the match, and you do not need to win a gammon, then there is no need to take any risks to win a gammon. Conversely, if losing the game loses the match you do not worry about being gammoned. You simply do everything possible to win the game.

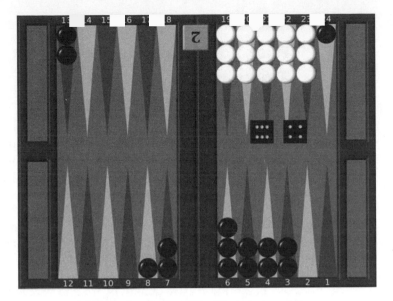

White leads 9 to 7 in 11-point match.
White owns 2-cube. Black to play 6-4

Under normal circumstances, Black should play 24/18, 13/9.
This almost ensures getting off the gammon. Black's odds of
winning from staying back are very small and there would be
significant gammon risk. White can make the ace point unless he
rolls a 6, and then if Black cannot enter reasonably quickly he will
be gammoned. At the actual score, Black should definitely stay back
and play 8/2, 6/2. Gammons are unimportant here: if Black loses
the game, he loses the match. While Black's chances of winning
from staying back may be small, they are much greater than if he
runs, since he is so far behind in the race.

Tip 39   Play Your First Backgammon Tournament

Backgammon tournaments can be a fun way to sharpen your skills, meet other backgammon players and perhaps even win a little bit of money in the process. Going to your first tournament can be a bit daunting because so many strange things seem to be happening, but it need not be.

Tournaments typically advertise two different times: the time that registration opens and the time that the tournament begins. Plan to arrive around the start of the registration period so that you have time to register, familiarize yourself with the rules and meet some of the other players. Bring a good quality board and precision dice if you have them, but there will be plenty available if you don't.

Every backgammon tournament has at least one tournament director, and many have more than one person helping with organization. When you first arrive, look for the registration table and go up and introduce yourself. Tell the person there that this is your first tournament, and they will be happy to walk you through the process.

Many tournaments have more than one division to choose from; there is often a beginner division and an open division, or sometimes beginner, intermediate and open divisions. Each division will have an entry fee. The tournament directors keep a portion of the entry fee to pay for the costs of running the tournament and the rest goes into the prize pool for that division. At your first tournament, you are almost certainly welcome to play in the beginner division. If you prove to be too skilled, the tournament director will politely invite you to move up to the next division on your next visit – and if this should happen, you are to be complimented on your achievement!

At the end of the registration period, the tournament directors will perform a random draw and put all of the names on a draw sheet. They will then either call out the first round pairings, or put the draw sheet on a wall so that you can find your opponent. Shortly after the tournament starts, they will announce what the total prize pool and prize distribution are for each division. In smaller tournaments only first or first and second place will receive prizes, but in larger fields it's common to pay several places.

Tournaments are often played as either a single elimination or double elimination format. In single elimination, each player is matched with an opponent for the first round and plays a match of the assigned length. The winner of that match advances to the next round, and the loser is eliminated from the tournament. In double elimination play, things begin as for single elimination. However, losing your first match does not eliminate you from the tournament. Instead, you move from the starting bracket (often called the winners' bracket) to a separate draw called the consolation bracket. You then continue to play within the consolation bracket until you lose another match. After losing a match in the consolation bracket you are eliminated from play. At the end of the tournament, the winner of the winners' bracket plays the winner of the consolation (losers') bracket. If the person from the winner's bracket wins, the tournament is over. Otherwise they play a second match to determine the final winner of the tournament.

Other types of format are used from time to time. If you have difficulty understanding the format for a particular tournament, simply ask the tournament director to explain it to you. Once a match starts, tell your opponent that this is your first tournament and ask them to let you know if you make any procedural mistakes. Most backgammon players are friendly and polite, and will be happy to help a beginner.

It is conventional for both players to record the score of the match, and to verbally check the score at the end of each game – 'it's three to two my favour, yes?' This allows you to catch errors early on, when they can more easily be resolved. If there are disputes about the score or anything else during the match, call the tournament director over and he or she will help you to resolve the problem.

At the end of the match, you should inform the tournament director who won. If you were the winner, the director will either tell you who your next opponent is, if known, or will let you know approximately a wait there is before your next match. If your have to wait, stay nearby and wait for your name to be called.

Once you are eliminated, you may find social or money games going on around the room, and you are welcome to join in. It is also generally acceptable to watch matches in progress, so long as you do so quietly without disrupting the players.

Tip 40   Understand the Crawford Rule

When a player has one point to go to win the match, it is obviously correct for his opponent to double as soon as legally possible, since the trailer has everything to gain and nothing to lose by doubling. But if the trailer were permitted to double immediately, this would considerably lessen the value of being one point away from winning the match.

In order to solve this problem, the late John Crawford came up with this rule: when a player reaches one point away from winning the match, there is no cube in the very next game only. This game is called the Crawford game. The trailer does score full value for a gammon or backgammon he might win in this game, but the cube remains at the 1-level. If the trailer wins that game and the match continues, he is permitted to double in the following games, and of course he should do so at his earliest opportunity.

The Crawford rule is commonly used in all tournaments today, as a good compromise that can lead to some interesting situations. For example, consider a Crawford game where a player has two points to go while his opponent has one point to go. Winning a gammon is extremely valuable for the trailer, here: if he wins a single game the match is tied, but if he wins a gammon he wins the entire match. A gammon is of no value at all to the leader, of course. Therefore, the trailer should be prepared to take considerable risks in order to win a gammon.

Under normal circumstances Black should play safe here, with 13/8, 7/4. Black is well ahead in the race and is very likely to win the game after this play. He could win a gammon if he plays 13/5*, but the risk is too great. If White hits back not only does White almost certainly win the game, but White might be the one winning the gammon.

At this match score, however, the circumstances are quite different. Black has just as much to gain from winning a gammon, as opposed to a single game, as he has to lose from turning his possible win into a loss. Getting gammoned is no concern to Black. If Black plays 13/5* and White flunks, Black has a good chance to close his board and win a gammon, and White will flunk 25/36 of the time. So in this situation it is correct to play 13/5*.

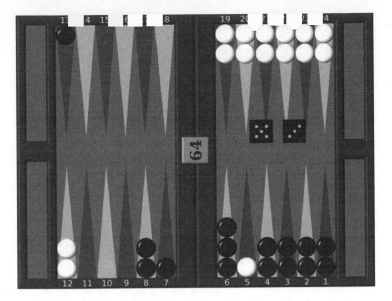

White leads 10-9, 11-point match, Crawford game.
Black to play 5-3

Now, suppose it is the Crawford game and the trailer has three points to go. If the trailer wins a single game he will double immediately next game, and that game (or the one after it, if the leader drops) will be for the match. If the trailer wins a gammon both players will have one point to go. Regardless of whether the trailer wins a single game or a gammon, the winner of the following game will win the match. Therefore gammons have virtually no value to the trailer and *both* players should play as though gammons are of no interest.

Since the trailer will be doubling as soon as he can after the Crawford game, this logic extends even further: if the trailer has an even number of points to go, winning a gammon is very important for him – because the extra point means he will need to win one fewer game than if he had only won a single game; however, if the trailer has an odd number of points to go, winning a gammon is ultimately of little value to him, since he will still need to win the same number of future games to win the match.

Tip 41 Use the Free Drop

It would appear at first glance that cube play after the Crawford game is trivial. The trailer will double at his first legal opportunity, since he has everything to gain and nothing to lose. The leader will have at worst almost an even game, so he should automatically take. But wait – things are not as simple as they seem.

Suppose that you are leading 10-9 in an 11-point match; your opponent won the Crawford game, and now he doubles you. If you take, you are playing this game for the match. But you are not required to take: your alternative is to pass, set the checkers up again and play for the match with the score 10-10. If you pass and play the next game for the match, you are clearly even money. Therefore, your decision of whether or not to take is simply this: you take if you are the favourite; you pass if you are the underdog.

Since your opponent will presumably double at his first legal opportunity, the double will come either on his first play, if you win the opening roll, or on his second play if he wins the opening roll. If you win the opening roll you should always take, regardless of what the opening roll actually is. Simply getting a head start in development and getting ahead in the race is sufficient to give you at least a small advantage, even if you get a poor opening roll.

If your opponent wins the opening roll, think again. Now he is the one who has the lead in development and in the race, and he gets to roll next. Under these circumstances, you would need to have rolled a much better number than he rolled to justify taking the double. For example, if you both roll 3-1 and each make your 5-points, and he now properly doubles, you should pass, because you are the underdog.

Now here is another example, with a slightly different score. This time you are ahead 10-8 in an 11-point match, post-Crawford, and your opponent doubles. If you take, he has to win both this game and the next game – assuming you do not get gammoned. What happens if you pass? He will double immediately on the next game and, whether or not you take, he will only have to win one game to win the match. Thus passing would be a huge blunder on your behalf – it would allow him to win the match by winning only one game instead of two games.

Carrying this a bit further, suppose you are ahead 10-7 in an 11-point match, post-Crawford, and your opponent doubles. If you take he has to win both this game and the next game (which he will also double immediately) to win the match, unless he wins a gammon – in which case he wins the match on this game. But if you pass the score will be 10-8; as we have seen, he again has to win two games, or one gammon, to win the match. Therefore you have a free drop available – you should pass if you are the underdog.

In general, if you are the underdog and your opponent has an even number of points to go, you can afford to drop – essentially, he will need to win the same number of games as he would if you had taken. If your opponent has an odd number of points to go, however, it would be a big blunder for you to drop – that would effectively reduce by one the number of games he needs to win.

We have been assuming that the trailer should always double at his first legal opportunity post-Crawford, but this may not necessarily be so. Suppose you are trailing and you have an even number of points to go. As we have seen, your opponent has a free drop available. If you get off to a great start, say a 3-1 by you and a 6-2 by him, it might be right for you to play on for a gammon without doubling: if things start to turn around you can always double, but if things continue to improve you can continue to play on and perhaps win a gammon if you are lucky. This policy should only be considered against a knowledgeable player who understands about the free drop, because a weak player may fail to understand and may take anyway.

What if you have an odd number of points to go? As already discussed, your opponent should always take – so it appears you might as well double. If your opponent understands the situation, you should double immediately. But if your opponent does not understand that he should virtually always take, you may be able to trap him. Instead of doubling immediately, wait until your game improves to the point where he would appear to have a drop. Now you double, and there is a possibility that he will blunder and pass.

The above strategies of not doubling immediately post-Crawford when trailing are very advanced and, unless you fully understand the concepts behind them, you would be well-advised to always double immediately.

Tip 42 Go All Out When Blitzing

One of the most effective ways to win a single game or a gammon is to run a successful blitz. You hit a couple of enemy checkers and they stay on the bar while you bring in the ammunition to continue attacking and making new points. If all goes as planned, you succeed in closing your opponent out and then waltz on home to victory.

When running a blitz, every builder is important. You need checkers in range to make points, or to hit if your opponent enters one of his men from the bar. The one thing you do not want is to allow your opponent the opportunity to make an anchor in your board. If he does that your blitz will fail, and often your game will fall apart. So once a blitz has started, it must operate as an all-out attack.

The huge importance of each new builder is much greater than might be thought. To provide an idea of why, consider the starting position and how many rolls are able to make the 5- or 4-point:

> 1-1: 5-point
> 2-2: 4-point
> 3-3: 5-point
> 4-4: either point
> 3-1: 5-point
> 4-2: 4-point

Those are the only rolls that can make these points – in fact, just 8 rolls out of 36 possibilities.

Now, put a checker on the 9-point and see how much this improves the matter. Now, in addition to the pointing rolls from the starting position, we have:

> 4-1: 5-point
> 4-3: 5-point
> 5-2: 4-point
> 5-4: 4-point

That provides 8 additional pointing rolls, thus doubling the number of rolls that make the 5- or 4-point – quite an improvement.

Now add a builder on the 10-point. In addition to the previous pointing rolls, we now have:

5-1: 5-point
5-3: 5-point
6-2: 4-point
6-4: 4-point
6-5: 4-point

That adds another 10 pointing rolls. In fact at this stage is getting difficult to find a roll that does not make a good point.

Since every new builder and attacker is so important, it is vital to bring them into range quickly. Your opponent may start to enter at any moment; you need to be poised to attack, and hopefully point on an entering checker. When running a blitz, almost all other considerations take a back seat to bringing in the ammunition.

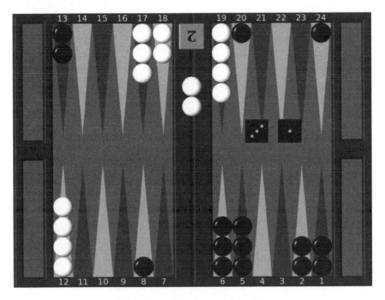

Blitzing. Black to play 3-1

Under normal circumstances it would be routine for Black to play 24/20, making the advanced anchor and advancing the back checker to where it is not hemmed in. But these are not normal circumstances: Black's correct play is 13/9, not only failing to make the advanced anchor but giving up the midpoint as well. The key is that Black is running an all-out blitz, and needs every builder in range either to pounce on any White checker that dares to enter or to make the fifth inner board point if White fails to enter. The midpoint is of no value, since Black will not need it if his blitz is successful. The anchor on White's 5-point is also unimportant, for the same reason. Black should have plenty of time to escape the back checker once he completes his closeout. What is important is to maximize the chances of completing the closeout, and that means bringing in every piece of ammunition right now. 13/9 is better than 24/23, 13/10, since the checker on the 9-point aims at the 3-point as well as the 4-point.

Tip 43
Bring in a Closed Board Safely

The ultimate offence in backgammon is a closed board with one or more enemy checkers on the bar. Your opponent cannot move, while you are free to move your remaining three checkers around the board wherever you want, in complete safety. A closeout will usually result in a victory, and often in a gammon. Still, it is important to be cautious and play carefully when you have a closed board. A bit of carelessness combined with some unlucky rolls can result in leaving a shot, and your opponent may snatch victory from the jaws of defeat.

If your opponent has any outfield points you must be aware of these stumbling blocks. If you leave a checker four or five pips away from an enemy point and then roll 4-4 or 5-5, you may be forced to break your closed board if unable to handle the roll with your other spare checkers. Be prepared for such rolls; place your checkers in such a way that there are no unlucky doubles that might force you to break your board prematurely.

The other thing to watch out for when bringing your checkers around is the 6-6 danger. If you are not careful, 6-6 will force you to leave a blot on the 6-point, with disastrous consequences. While it is not worth playing an ugly move, such as dumping your spares onto lower points in order to avoid leaving a shot on 6-6, do play so as not to leave a shot if this is conveniently possible. This is the only roll you have to worry about when you have checkers in the outfield. If 6-6 plays safely, everything will play safely.

Consider where you should best put your checkers when you bring them home. It might seem correct to put a checker on the 6-point for more flexibility, but this is not the right idea. What you are aiming for is to have just two checkers on the 6-point, with spares on the middle points. This way, once you have brought everybody home you can clear the 6-point safely with any roll. The worst structure is to have three checkers on the 6-point with only two on the 5-point. Now big doubles and 6-5 will leave a shot, and if the lower points also have only two checkers, there are even more rolls that leave a shot. You should generally aim to put the first checker to be brought home onto the 5-point. From there it can later be moved or left where it is, depending upon the dice roll. After that, the next checker is best on the 4-point.

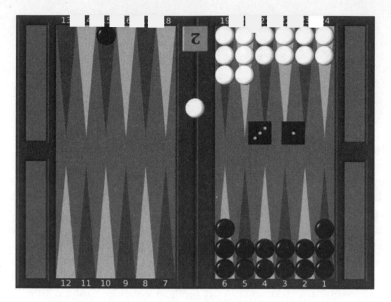

Bringing in a closed board (1). Black to play 3-1

It might seem fine to play 15/11, getting home as quickly as possible – but there is danger lurking. Suppose Black does play 15/11 and his next roll is 5-4. Now he will have to play 11/2 (11/7, 6/1 is even worse). This leaves Black with three checkers on the 6-point and the 5-, 4- and 3-points stripped. Black leaves a shot on the next roll if he rolls 6-6, 5-5, 6-5, 6-4 or 6-3. In addition, in order to play safely with a roll such as 5-3 Black will be forced to clear the 5-point while he still has checkers on the 6-point, and this gap may produce shots later.

Black's proper play with the 3-1 is 15/12, 6/5. This strips the 6-point so that Black is prepared to clear it once he gets all his checkers home. Now if Black rolls 5-4 he plays 12/3, and then only 6-6 or 5-5 leave a shot next turn. With other rolls he can clear the 6-point, which is what he wants to do.

After getting everybody home, the general policy is to clear from the back as quickly as possible while leaving spares on the middle points to help handle awkward rolls. A stripped position can be dangerous.

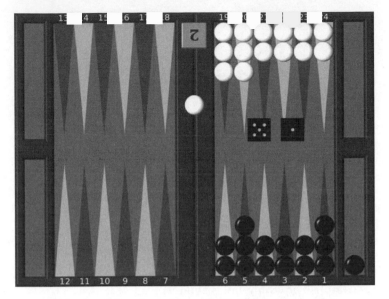

Bringing in a closed board (1). Black to play 5-1

It may seem routine to rip two checkers off, but a stripped position is dangerous. There will be no problem if Black rolls large numbers – but what if Black takes two checkers off and then rolls 6-1? He will be forced to play 6/0, 6/5, leaving three checkers on the 5-point and two on every other point. This is as dangerous a position as there could be, because any subsequent roll that contains a 6 or a 5 will leave a shot. Instead, Black should play 6/5, 6/1. This lets White in early, which is good for Black: once White is in, Black is completely safe. If White stays out, Black will still have four checkers on the 5-point and can move two of them next roll, which will also leave a pretty safe position.

It should be noted that if the gammon race is close it may be correct to take slight risks in order to hold the closed board longer. But when the gammon is very unlikely (as in the above position) or when the gammon is a virtual certainty if a shot is not hit, then safety is your number one priority.

Tip 44   Diversify Your Good Numbers

Since you cannot control what you roll, one of your main goals is to maximize the number of good rolls you will have for upcoming turns, by leaving a variety of 'good numbers' on different parts of the board. If rolling a 3 is good in relation to one part of the board, it is inefficient for it to also be good for another part of the board. It is better if rolling some other number, say a 4, is good elsewhere, because this will mean that you can do something beneficial if you either roll a 3 or a 4 next, and if you happen to roll 4-3 you can do twice as much. Conversely, if 3s are needed in both places, you will not accomplish anything unless you roll a 3.

Any of the actions described below will improve your position. And by diversifying the numbers that accomplish these goals, you leave yourself more good rolls.

> Making an advanced anchor
> Moving a back checker to where it can escape
> Springing a back checker out
> Hitting an enemy blot
> Covering a blot of your own
> Making a new inner board point or blocking point

It is not always clear what your good numbers will be. Your opponent, of course, takes his roll after you play and his move may alter your priorities. For example, if he has a blot that you would like to hit, there is a good chance that he will either move or cover that blot, so your planned good hitting number will no longer exist. Still, you will usually know what you are trying to accomplish and what your good numbers will be.

If your opponent is on the bar there is some chance that he will flunk, which will leave the position exactly the same as it was after you make your current move. In this case you may be able to plan your good numbers for next turn, on the optimistic assumption that the position will probably remain unchanged.

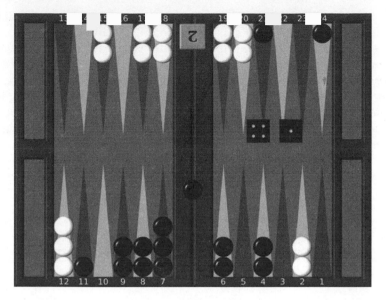

Diversification. Black to play 4-1

Black will enter with the 4, of course, and he has to choose the best ace to play. Since he is not going to break a point, his choices are 24/23, 11/10 and 7/6. At first glance this choice might seem random, but it is actually quite important. Black needs to choose the ace that will diversify his good numbers as much as possible. Let us see what Black needs to be doing with his checkers:

Black needs to advance his back checker up to the 22-point or the 21-point. It can escape with a 5 from the 21-point, and with a 6 from the 22-point, but it cannot escape directly from the 23-point or the 24-point. So that checker has good 2s and 3s where it is now. If it is advanced to the 23-point, it will have good 1s and 2s.

Black's checkers on the 21-point need 5s to escape. It is quite important for Black to escape a checker. White has better timing than Black with those three checkers on the midpoint, so if Black does not escape soon he may be forced to break his blockade.

On the offensive front, it is quite clear what Black should do: he needs to make his 5-point in order to solidify his blockade. At the moment he is willing to give up his 9-point to make the 5-point, since White is not directly threatening the 9-point, but he will not give up his 8-point, since that point blocks White's 6s. As things are now, Black can make his 5-point with a combination of 2s, 4s and 6s. If Black plays 11/10, he makes the 5-point with a combination of 2s, 4s and 5s. If he plays 7/6, he makes the 5-point with a combination of 1s, 4s and 6s.

So, which ace should Black play? Clearly, 11/10 is wrong: Black has good 5s on the other side of the board, and by staying back on the 11-point he leaves himself good 6s. If Black plays 24/23, he gives himself good 2s on both sides of the board, which is not ideal in terms of diversification. The best ace is 7/6. This leaves Black good 2s, 3s and 5s on White's side of the board and combinations of 1s, 4s and 6s to make the 5-point. That move diversifies Black's good numbers as much as possible, and maximizes his chances of getting a favourable roll next turn.

Tip 45   Duplicate Your Opponent's Good Numbers

It is just as important to minimize your opponent's good rolls as it is to maximize your own. You want to force your opponent to be unlucky: by giving your opponent fewer good rolls, you improve your chances of winning the game.

There are six possible numbers for an individual die. Each number your opponent can actually play optimizes his number of good rolls. For example, if he has a good 2 to play and a good 3 to play, then any roll which contains a 2 or a 3 will be favourable to him. It is as though he has a double shot where he can hit with a 2 or a 3. On the other hand, if only a 3 will play favourably for him, he will not have as many good rolls.

The idea behind duplication is to make your move in such a way that your opponent has the same good number at different places on the board. If he does not roll that number, he will not have a good roll. The most obvious example is when you are forced to leave your opponent more than one shot, and he wants to hit very much. If you leave him the same number to hit in both places, he will have fewer hitting numbers.

When considering a duplication play, it is important that your opponent wants equally to use the number in question in both places. If his gain in one place would be much greater than his gain in the other place, then the duplication does not do much good. Many players make this mistake and leave unnecessary shots because they involve duplication, when the alternative way the opponent can play the duplicated number is not nearly as important as hitting the shot. But when both options open to him are very important to your opponent, duplication can be quite effective.

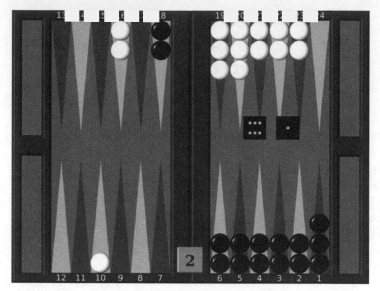

Duplication (1). Black to play 6-1

Black would rather have rolled anything but this, because now he is forced to expose both blots. He must make the best of a bad situation. If he holds his board and plays 18/11, he leaves White 1s and 2s with which to hit, as well as 5-3 and 4-4. Playing 18/12, 18/17 is just as bad, because it is vital to minimize White's shot-hitting numbers. So, instead, Black should duplicate Whites 2s by playing 18/12, 6/5, even though this costs Black his perfect board. By leaving White 2s to hit in both places, he has ensure that White has fewer rolls that hit. Now rolls 6-1, 5-1, 4-1 and 3-1 do not hit, while they would have if Black had played 18/11.

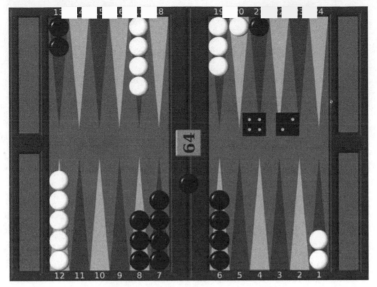
Duplication (2). Black to play 4-2

Here, Black will enter with the 4, of course, and must then find the best 2 to play. He is not going to break his midpoint and leave a direct shot there, whereas 8/6 is safe but ugly. Since White's board is weak and Black has an advanced anchor, this is a good opportunity to slot a key inner board point. The natural-looking play is 7/5, slotting the more valuable 5-point. But if Black thinks in terms of duplication, 6/4 is actually superior. The key is that White very much needs to cover the blot on his 5-point, so 3s are already quite good for him. By playing 6/4, Black duplicates those 3s, making a 3 the best number for White on both sides of the board – giving White somewhat of a dilemma. If Black instead plays 7/5 he creates a good 4 for White, thus greatly increasing White's good rolls. This is sufficient to compensate for the value of slotting the 5-point versus the 4-point.

Tip 46

Make the Move Your Opponent Does Not Want You to Make

You will often be faced with a choice of moves in which the best move is not clear. There are various approaches you might take that could improve your position and each of these approaches will have different risks. How to evaluate these risks and rewards is often unclear.

A good way to analyze such a problem is to mentally 'walk around to the other side of the board', to see how things look from the other side. Consider what move you would *not* like to see made, were you to be in your opponent's shoes. Find the move that you would be the most uncomfortable with, and that is the move you should be making: the move your opponent does not want you to make. Incidentally, this advice is quite applicable to all games of skill, not just backgammon.

The following position is a good example of how focusing on what the other person does not want to see can lead you to a move that you might not have even been considered otherwise:

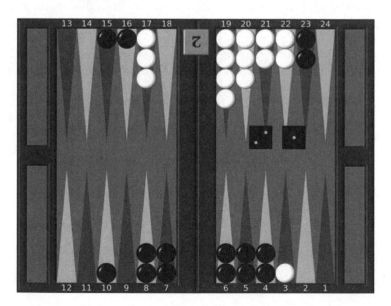

Choose the move your opponent hates.
Black to play 2-1

What should Black be trying to do here – should he block 6-6 with 16/15, 10/8 perhaps, block 6-5 with 16/14, 15/14, maybe diversify builders to make the 9-point with 16/13 or even prepare to attack White's blot with 10/7? All of these possibilities look reasonable, but nothing seems particularly decisive.

Try mentally moving over to White's side of the board, to see how things look – not at all bad, actually: all White needs to do is roll a 6 and he is out in the clear. Even if White fails to roll a 6 immediately he still has a strong blockade, as well as checkers that he can move so as to retain his blockade while waiting to roll his 6 in the next couple of rolls. If Black hits White on the 3-point, White might hit back and still retain his blockade. None of the possible plays suggested so far will bother White much.

Now, suppose Black plays 16/14, 10/9. White is not so happy about things now. Yes, if White rolls a 6 he will hit and also be in a good position, but he would be in a good position if he rolls a 6, regardless of what Black does. And suppose White does *not* roll that 6. In this scenario Black will have 6s, 5s and various combinations (4-2, 4-1, 3-2, 3-3, 2-2) to make the 9-point and complete a full prime. Once Black has made the prime, all he will need to do is roll a 5 to escape one back checker and the game will be his. White's board will be forced to crunch. Moreover, even if Black does not roll that 5 immediately he will still have one free checker in the outfield to play with, and White will have to continue playing his rolls as well, with a decent chance that White will have to release some of his blockade before Black is forced to break his prime.

Obviously White does not want to see Black slot the edge of the prime and put the pressure on White to roll a 6 immediately. And since this is not what White wants to see, this is exactly the move that Black should make.

Tip 47
Good Rolls Are Made, Not Born

Backgammon is a dice game: there is an element of chance involved, so your choice of moves is limited by the numbers that you roll. But if you watch an expert, it often appears as though he is getting more than his share of good rolls. This is not down to having particularly good luck – he gets the same rolls as everybody else. The difference is that the expert has positioned his checkers so that more rolls will play well. Good rolls are not born: they are made by proper placement of the checkers.

If a player has all his checkers stacked on a few points, he is at the mercy of the dice; if the dice do not cooperate with a lucky roll he will not be able to improve his game. On the other hand, if he keeps his checkers spread out then he will have more ways to play his move and thus more lucky rolls. Of course one must be somewhat discreet, since every blot is a potential target. However, it is generally correct to leave an indirect shot in order to get an extra builder.

Every builder makes a big difference. For example, consider the starting position. The only non-doubles that make a new point are 3-1, 4-2, 5-3, 6-4 and 6-1. Moving one of the checkers off the midpoint to the 9-point brings quite a bit of improvement:

> 2-1 makes the bar point
> 4-1 makes the 5-point
> 4-3 makes the 5-point
> 5-2 makes the 4-point
> 5-4 makes the 4-point
> 6-2 makes the bar point
> 6-3 makes the 3-point
> 6-5 makes the 3-point

In fact, 5-1 and 3-2 are the only non-doubles that fail to make a new point. This example illustrates just how powerful one extra builder can be, proving just how easy it is to be lucky when almost all of your possible rolls play well.

The following example illustrates how careful play can give you more lucky rolls:

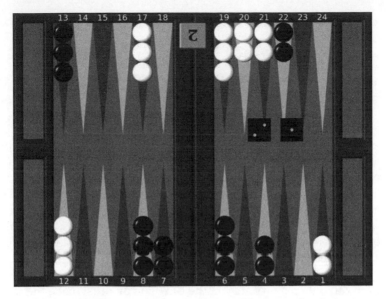

Good rolls are made, not born. Black to play 2-1

Black wants very much to make his 5-point. Unfortunately, playing 7/5, 6/5 loses the bar point and leaves a direct shot there, which is too much to give away. Also, slotting the 5-point with 8/5 leaves a direct shot. Black can play safe with 8/7, 6/4, but that loses the vital spare on the 6-point. So Black should play either 13/10 or 13/11, 8/7 – the problem is which. It would appear that 13/11, 8/7 is best. The key is that Black is willing to give up his 8-point in order to make the 5-point, since he would be left with a solid 4-prime and would leave only an indirect shot. After 13/11, 8/7 Black can make his 5-point next roll and keep a 4-prime with any of 1-1, 2-1, 3-1, 6-1, 2-2, 3-2, 6-2, 3-3 and 6-3. After 13/10, he can make his 5-point and keep a 4-prime only with 1-1, 3-1, 5-1, 3-3 and 5-3. As you can see, proper checker placement will give you a lot more good rolls.

Tip 48   Do not Waste Pips When Getting Off Gammon

While it is nice to try to win the game, sometimes winning is out of the question. The best you can do then is scramble all your men home in order to take a checker off and avoid getting gammoned. Remember, when running to avoid a gammon, the only objective is to bring *all* of your men into your inner board so you can take *one* checker off. Bringing just some of your men home is not good enough, and taking more than one checker off will not matter – but all the checkers must get into the inner board. Achieving this efficiently can mean the difference between losing a single game and losing a double game.

You can only play what is on the dice, so you must make the most of what you roll. If you bring a checker inside beyond the 6-point, you have wasted those pips. The most efficient way to bring the outfield checkers home is to put them all on the 6-point. That way, every pip can be utilized for moving the outfield checkers around the board. Every pip counts – wasting a single pip might be the difference between getting gammoned and not getting gammoned.

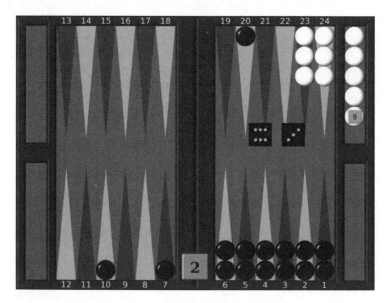

Do not waste pips (1). Black to play 6-3

In this example, assuming that White does not roll doubles, Black will have two more rolls to get off the gammon. His proper play is 20/11: this does not waste any pips and poises his three outfield checkers so that two of them can be brought home next roll. On the following roll, hopefully Black will be able to bring the third checker home with one of the dice and take a checker off with the other. For example, if Black's next roll is 5-1, he will play 11/6, 7/6. Then all he needs is a 4 or better on one of the dice to bring the checker on the 10-point home and take a man off.

Look at the difference if Black mistakenly plays 20/14, 7/4. This brings a checker home, but wastes two vital pips. Now if Black follows with 5-1, the best he can do is to play 14/8. After that, he will need 2-2, or larger doubles, in order to take a checker off on the following roll.

The priorities may change if Black absolutely needs to take a checker off on the next roll. Now it is simply a matter of counting and seeing which rolls will work next turn.

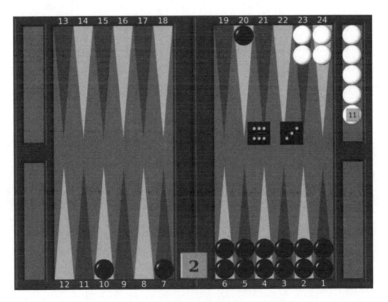

Do not waste pips (2). Black to play 6-3

This time Black does not have two rolls. He must take a checker off next turn, since White needs at most two rolls to bear everybody off. If Black plays 20/11, he can take a checker off next turn only if he rolls 5-5 or 6-6. Rolling 4-4 will not be good enough because he will need all four 4s to bring his men into his inner board. On the other hand, if Black plays 20/14, 7/4, then 4-4 next turn just makes it –

14/6, 10/6, 4/0. So in this position 20/14, 7/3 is the proper play, even though it wastes two pips. There is no rule of thumb for this sort of position where you need to get off on the next roll. You simply have to examine all plays and count the rolls needed to make each one successful.

Tip
49

Timing is Everything in a Priming Battle

Hitting an enemy blot and sending it to the bar is usually a good thing to do, because you not only force your opponent to enter, you also take away half of his roll. If he is unable to enter you will have done even better, by making him forfeit his entire turn.

There are certain positions where the opposite is true, and you actually want your opponent to be forced to play his roll. This can occur when he has a strong board or blockade but has few or no spare checkers to play with. If he is on the bar, he does not have to play if he is unable to enter, which is a good situation for him when he is trying to maintain a precarious position. If he is not on the bar he has to play his full roll, which is good for you.

So, in this sort of position, normal principles are reversed. Hitting an enemy blot becomes bad for you and good for your opponent. Conversely, if you are trying to hold a board together it may be good for you to be hit. The game becomes a stalling battle instead of a race, and the player who can hold out the longest will be the winner.

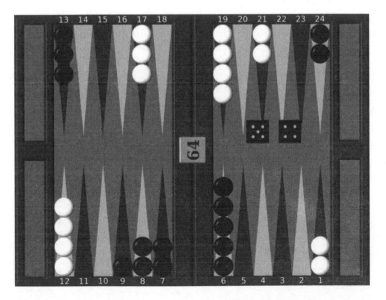

Figure 49.1 Priming battle. Black to play 5-4

Black is in trouble. He is behind a full prime; so long as White is able to hold that prime, Black will be unable to escape. Instead he will be forced to play on his side of the board, which means that his position will soon crumble. The only way Black can prevent this happening is by forcing White to break the prime.

At first glance, 5-4 looks like a perfect roll for Black, making the 2-point on White's head and completing both a 5-point board and a full prime. Under normal circumstances, that would be the case, but these are not normal circumstances. White has a full prime; if Black makes the 2-point on White's head, White will remain on the bar most of the time and is only forced to enter if he rolls an ace. Even if White does roll an ace, he can handle 1-2 and 1-3 and still keep his full prime. So while making the 2-point looks pretty, it is not a winning strategy.

Black's best shot is to make the unusual-looking play of 7/3, 6/1. This is his best chance to force White to break the prime. If White rolls a 6, that is just too bad. More often than not White will not roll that 6, and then things may get interesting. White has a few small numbers that hold the prime together, but any 4 or 5 that does not contain a 6, as well as all doubles other than 6-6, force White to break the prime. Once White has been forced to break the prime, Black has a fighting chance. He can escape if he rolls the right escaping number, and if he is unable to escape he may be able to attack White's back checker. The key is to force White to break that prime, because as long as White holds the prime, Black can do nothing. Hitting is counter-productive: White must not be put on the bar, rather he must be forced to play his full roll.

Tip 50   Know How to Walk a Prime Home

One of the greatest feelings in backgammon comes when you have your opponent trapped behind a full prime – a solid block of six consecutive points. As long as you retain the prime, a trapped checker cannot escape. Your opponent will be forced to play elsewhere, crunching his board, while you are free to move at will. Unless your opponent has or is able to form a prime of his own, you have no fears. It does not matter if he hits a blot because if you get stuck on the bar, that is fine by you. You do not have to move and he does, which means that your prime remains intact while his deteriorates until it reaches the point where he will have to let you enter.

But all good things must come to an end. Twelve checkers are needed for the prime, so that leaves you with only three checkers to play with. You have to keep moving, and eventually you will have to move one of the checkers in the prime; then, if you are not careful, your opponent may be able to escape. What you would like to do is to advance the prime forward, retaining the solid prime at all times, until it becomes a closed board with your opponent on the bar. After that, all you need to do is bear off safely and you have an almost certain victory.

How should the prime be advanced? Well, you want to make the next point in the prime, but you do not need to roll a perfect number to make this point – you can afford to slot it. As we have seen, it will not hurt if you are hit. You just enter again and send another checker to slot the point, and eventually you roll a number to cover it. You can cover from the back with a 6, or you can cover with one of your other free checkers. Covering from the back with a 6 is fine, since the back point of the prime is no longer needed once the prime is advanced. Simply repeat this slot and cover routine until you have walked the prime home to a closed board.

It is important to slot the front edge of the prime as quickly as possible. The fastest way to make a point is to slot it, and it does not matter if the slotted checker is hit. If you fool around and fail to slot it quickly, the dice may fail to cooperate when you need them to. You may be forced to break the prime, after which your opponent could roll a lucky number to escape the prime and win.

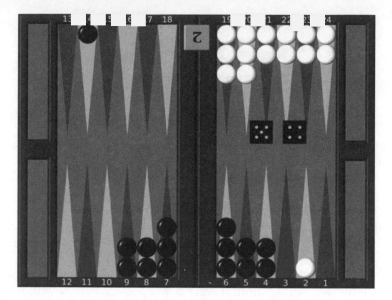

Walking a prime off. Black to play 5-4

In this example Black wants to advance his prime. Making the 2-point on White's head would be an error because this would take two vital builders away from the 3-point, essentially putting those checkers out of play. After making the 2-point, Black would have to roll well to make the 3-point. Black could make the 3-point right now with 8/3, 7/3, but that would break the prime and give White 6s to hit and escape, so of course Black cannot do that. Playing 14/5 looks natural, giving Black a new and well-placed builder for the 3-point, but if Black rolls something containing a 5, 1 or various doubles, he will be unable to advance his prime next roll. The star play is 14/9, 7/3, which gives Black 6s and 3s to make the 3-point and walk the prime forward. If Black fails to cover, things could get awkward, but this is by far Black's best chance to make the 3-point while retaining the prime. Even though White has a closed board, Black will not care if White hits. Black cannot move and White cannot escape while Black's prime is in place, so White would have to continue to roll until he broke some inner board points and Black entered.

Tip 51   Be Willing to Shift Points

When you make a good inner board point, there is a natural tendency to think of this point as a fixed asset. That point is going to remain until you are bearing off your checkers – this is the natural course of events and will usually be what happens.

The 6-point is generally the most valuable of the inner board points, followed by the 5-point, etc., and there are several reasons why the farther-out points are more valuable.

1) If your opponent is on the bar, these points make it more difficult for him to enter and escape. If he enters on a low point, he still has to escape. If he enters on a high point, his escape route is clear.

2) These points not only serve to prevent a hit checker from entering, but they also form part of a potential prime or blockade. Low points are effective if your opponent is on the bar, but once he has entered, the points lose their value if they are behind the entering checker.

3) The higher points serve as good landing places when you are bearing in to take your checkers off.

4) The higher points are places where you can put builders that can be used later to make the lower points.

For these reasons, any release of a higher point in favour of a lower point must be made with care. However, there are positions where it is profitable to switch to a lower point. These positions usually involve hitting an enemy checker, although switching in order to swallow an awkward number may also be a reason for switching. It may also be beneficial to switch to a lower point in order to fill in a gap before bearing off, if your opponent is on the bar or holding a low point on your home board. You'll be clearing that high point shortly anyway, and it may be worth shifting to a lower point if you can clear the high one safely.

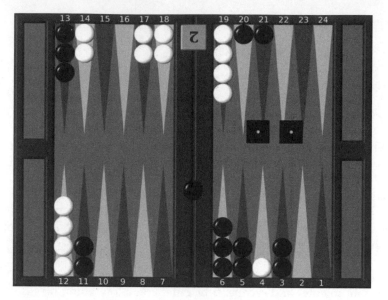

Shifting points (2). Black to play 1-1

Here, Black will certainly use two of the 1s from his double to enter and make White's 5-point. That defensive anchor ensures that Black will stay in the game, whatever happens. The other two 1s will be used to improve Black's offence. Moving 11/10(2) is an improvement, since it blocks White's escaping 6s, but White still has plenty of possible rolls which do escape. So it is better to hit White's blot and make it more difficult to escape. The natural-looking play is 6/4*, but this has some drawbacks: it leaves a direct shot, the 6-point is stripped and there is no builder in direct range to cover the blot on the 4-point.

A better play is to switch with 6/5(2)*. The 4-point is not quite as strong as the 5-point, but it is almost as good. This play leaves no direct shots from the bar and also keeps the vital spare on the 6-point. In addition, it activates the checkers on the 11-point, since they now bear down on the empty 5-point. This makes them more useful than when the 5-point was already made.

Shifting plays can be difficult to find, partly because the mental fixation on 'once a point, always a point' makes these plays easy to overlook. So try to stay flexible in your thinking and you may see some unexpected possibilities, which can be very profitable. But do not overdo it – low points are not as good as higher points.

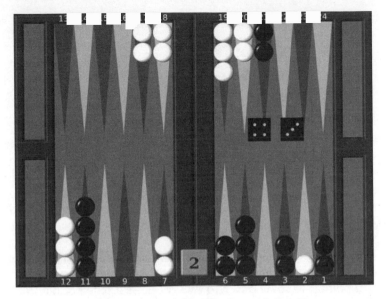

Shifting points (2). Black to play 4-3

How can Black play the 4? If he plays 5/1 he buries a checker, and then his only 3 will be 11/8, which leaves a double shot. He would like to hit with the 3, but that leaves him no 4. So it looks like all that is left is 11/4, which at least slots a good point, but leaves a direct shot and does nothing to molest White's lone back checker.

If Black is willing to think in terms of possibly giving up his 6-point, he will see that there is a 4 if he hits with the 3. Playing 6/2*, 5/2 is not bad at all: it puts White on the bar against a 4-point board, which threatens to get something going.

If White flunks, Black will have a chance to remake his 6-point, and then there is a decent chance that White will stay on the bar for a while, giving Black the opportunity to escape the back checkers. If White enters with a 6 and hits, Black's game will fall apart – but he is already in pretty bad shape with this roll. By putting White on the bar, Black gives himself the chance of improving his situation.

Tip 52

Clear from the Back

When bearing off against a deep anchor, safety is generally the number one priority. Taking checkers off is not too important because you are already way ahead in the race. The one thing you want to avoid if possible is leaving a shot. Unfortunately, you cannot simply rely on the dice to be cooperative. Instead, your goal should be to play in such a way that the chances of leaving shots are minimized.

In order to bear the checkers off, each point needs to be cleared. Unless you are fortunate enough to roll doubles, the only way to clear a point is to come down to two checkers on the point and then roll a number that allows you to move both the checkers. If you are unable to move both the checkers, you will need to find another way to play your roll.

Avoid gaps in your board. Every gap is one less safe landing place for the checkers on the point you are trying to clear. For example, suppose your opponent owns your ace point and you own your 2-, 3-, 4-, 5- and 6-points. Naturally you will come down to two checkers on the 6-point and hope to clear it. The only number that cannot be played from the 6-point is a 5. Any roll that does not contain a 5 will allow you to clear the 6-point safely. But suppose you have a gap on your 4-point. Now 2s cannot play safely from the 6-point (without becoming a blot), so you need to roll two numbers that contain neither a 5 nor a 2. In addition, once you clear the 6-point you will have the problem of clearing the 5-point safely, and due to the gap on the 4-point 1s will not play safely from the 5-point. If the gap had instead been on the 5-point that would not have been so bad, since once the 6-point is cleared there will be no gap. Thus, gaps on lower points are worse than gaps on higher points.

Since gaps are bad, the game plan is to clear from the back. Come down to two checkers on the highest point, roll a number that clears the checkers from it, and then repeat the process. While doing this, you want to keep spares on the next highest point or two, in order to swallow bad rolls. For example, when coming in against an ace-point anchor, suppose you come down to two checkers on the 6-point and roll a 5-4. You cannot play the 5 from the 6-point, and of course you prefer not to play 6/2 with the 4 since that would leave a shot. If you have a spare on the 5- and 4-points, you can play 5/0, 4/0 safely. But if one of these points does not have a third checker, there will be no safe way to play the roll.

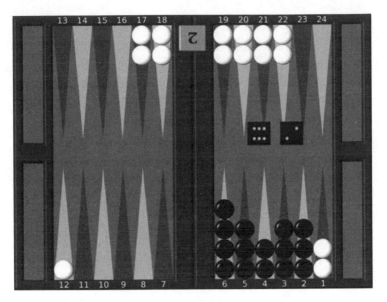

Clear from the back. Black to play 6-2

White has a very strong board, so Black's sole goal here is to avoid leaving a shot. Throwing 6-2 may seem like an ideal roll, since it allows Black to take two checkers off – and it is, but only if played properly. The correct play is 6/0, 6/4. This strips the 6-point down to two checkers, which is what Black is trying to do, and, in addition, puts an important spare on the 4-point. While it is true that if Black rolls 6-5, 6-6 or 4-4 after this play he will be forced to leave a shot, that is not important. The 6-5 risk will always be there once Black comes down to two checkers on the 6-point, and unless Black is fortunate enough to roll doubles he will have to come down to two checkers on the 6-point in order to clear the point safely. The important thing is to get down to two checkers on the 6-point as quickly as possible, while there are still spares on the 5- and 4-points to handle the awkward rolls. If Black delays stripping the 6-point he may find himself in a completely stripped position, having two checkers on each of the 6, 5 and 4-points. If Black were to roll 6-5 or 5-4 then it would be much worse, since with no spares on the 5- or 4-points he would be forced to leave two blots.

Glossary

Ace
The number one.

Ace point
The lowest point on the home board. An ace-point game is one in which one player has two or more checkers on his opponent's 1-point late in the game, often because they have never been moved.

Anchor
A point occupied by two or more checkers in the opponent's home board. An advanced anchor is one in which the anchor is on the 4-point or 5-point, or in very rare situations the 6-point.

Back game
A game in which two or more anchors are held in the opponent's home board, late in the game. A back game is typically played when the player is substantially behind in the race, and hopes to win by hitting one or more shots and then containing the hit checker(s) behind a prime.

Backgammon
A game in which the losing player still has checkers left in his opponent's home board and has not yet borne off any checkers. Backgammon is scored as three points, or three times the value of the doubling cube. (Also, of course, backgammon is the game that is the topic of this book.)

Back man
The two checkers that start the game in the opponent's home board, or any checker that ends up there during the course of the game.

Bar
The divider between the home board and the outer board, running down the middle of the backgammon board. When checkers are hit during play they are placed on the bar and remain there until they enter.

Bar point

The 7-point, the point closest to the bar in the outer board.

Bear in

To bring checkers into the home board.

Bear Off

To remove checkers from the board towards the end of the game.

Beaver

A rule sometimes used in money play, but never in match play, that allows the player accepting the doubling cube to instantly double again, while still maintaining possession of the cube.

Blitz

An aggressive attack on opponent checkers in the home board as an attempt to close them out.

Blot

A single checker on a point that is vulnerable to being hit.

Board

The backgammon playing area. Also, refers to one of the quadrants of the playing surface. In the second sense backgammon playing board has four separate boards when in use, called the inner and outer boards, for each side. See Inner board and Outer board.

Builder

A spare checker on a point, or a blot, that is in position to make an important point.

Closed Board

A home board that has all six points closed. A closed board is valuable because a checker that is hit has no way to enter.

Communication

Keeping checkers within six spaces of each other so that they can make points and protect each other.

Crawford rule

A rule used in match play that forbids the doubling cube from being used in the first game after one player's points total reaches exactly one point away from winning the match.

Crossover
Crossing from one quadrant to another in the process of bringing a checker home. For example, moving a checker from your outer board to your inner board is a crossover.

Cube
See Doubling cube.

Dance
Rolling a number that fails to enter a checker that is on the bar. Backgammon players have many creative names for this – dance, fan, flunk – not to mention quite a few that cannot be used in polite company.

Direct shot
A blot that is six or fewer spaces in front of an opponent's checker. A direct shot can be hit by playing a number from only one die.

Double
To offer to double the stakes of the game by turning the doubling cube. Also, in an entirely different sense, rolling the exact same number on both dice (as in 'throwing a double').

Doubling cube
A six-sided die that is marked with the numbers 2-4-8-16-32-64. This is used to raise the stakes of the game at various points.

Drop
To decline a double that is offered. Also resign, reject.

Fan
See dance.

Flunk
See dance.

Forced play
A roll for which there is only one legal move.

Gammon
A game in which the losing player has not borne off any checkers at the end of the game. A gammon is scored at two points, or twice the value of the doubling cube.

Gammoned
To lose a gammon, and lose twice the value of the doubling cube.

Hit
To land on a point occupied by an opponent's blot. Hitting an opponent's checker sends it to the bar.

Hit loose
To hit an opponent's blot and leave your own blot in its place, where it is subject to being hit on the following roll.

Home board
The quadrant of the board that contains a player's 1-6-points. All checkers must be moved to the player's home board before they can be borne off. Also called the inner board.

Indirect shot
A blot that is more than six spaces away, but can be hit by using both numbers of a dice roll.

Inner board
See Home board.

Jacoby rule
A rule that says that gammons and backgammons are only worth one point unless the doubling cube has been offered and accepted during that game. The Jacoby rule is sometimes used in money play, but never in match play.

Leader
In match play, the person who is ahead in the match score.

Make a point
To place two or more checkers on a single point. When a point is made, the opponent's checkers cannot land on it.

Market
The window of opportunity during which your opponent will accept a double if you turn the cube. If you wait until you have too big an advantage and your opponent will drop, then you are said to have lost your market.

Match
A series of games that is played until one player reaches a

predetermined score. For example, a 7-point match ends when one player has scored 7 or more points, regardless of the opponent's score.

Midpoint
A player's 13-point. At the start of each game, there are five checkers on the midpoint.

Money play
A sequence of backgammon games that are scored and tallied individually. The winner is the one who has scored the most points when playing stops. If the games are being played for a wager, the loser then pays the winner the amount of the wager multiplied by the difference in the score. For example, if the final score was 13-7, the loser would pay the winner six points.

Outer board
The quadrant of the board that contains the player's 7-12-points.

Outfield
The outer board.

Pass
To drop an offered double. Also, a position in which the correct play is to drop the double if it is offered.

Pip
One spot on a die.

Pip count
The total number of pips that a player must roll in order to move all of his checkers home and then bear them off.

Point
The name given to each of the 24 triangles on the board on which checkers can be placed (as in 1-point, 2-point, etc). Also, in the sense of scoring points, the value of a single game of backgammon.

Prime
Several consecutive points on the board that are all held by a player, most commonly on his side of the board. Enemy checkers can be trapped behind a prime, and it will be difficult or impossible for them to escape until the prime is broken.

Race

The relative standing of the players' pip counts, used to determine who is closest to bearing all their checkers off. Also, a position in which contact has been broken and there is no longer an opportunity for either player to hit the other's checkers.

Recube

To offer the doubling cube in a position where you own the cube.

Rip off

To bear off as many checkers as possible on a roll.

Run

Advancing a checker with the primary purpose of gaining ground in the race.

Slot

To place a single checker on a point, in the hope of making that point on a subsequent roll.

Split

To separate two checkers that are on a point, leaving two blots. This is most commonly done with the back men.

Stack

To place more than two checkers on a single point. Unstacking is removing extra checkers from a point.

Take

To accept an offered double. Also, a position in which the correct play is to accept a double if it is offered.

Tempo

Half of a dice roll. When you hit your opponent and send him to the bar, it costs him a tempo (half of his next roll) to enter, which hinders his ability to make strategic plays.

Trailer

In match play, the person who is behind in the match score.

Index